What leaders are saying about "Precept Upon Precept."

While gathering information for a bible study on the book of Revelation, I was offered a copy of "Precept Upon Precept." Of all the books I've purchased, I found none as insightful. It has challenged and aided me in how I interpret scripture.

> *Shundrawn A. Thomas, Book Store Owner, Author and Minister, Chicago Ill.*

The manuscript of this book was given to me so that I could review it. Before long I found myself underlining especially insightful sections. I soon forgot why I was reading this manuscript – I was simply being spiritually fed.

I believe most Christians would like to know their Bible better. They would like to be motivated by its message but often find themselves bogged down with too much information that is difficult to understand. Virgil has taken the first half of the Bible, the Old Testament, and tied its history and prophecy of Jesus together to give us a comprehensive (yet simple) understanding of the Book of Revelation. Every Bible scholar and new Christian should read and own a copy of Precept Upon Precept.

Reader, you are about to devour a book which will have an impact on your relationship with God. You will find yourself highlighting scriptures which were once difficult to understand but now make perfect sense.

Virg, thank you for your clarity in addressing questions (relating to the Book of Revelation) which <u>all</u> Christians want to understand. Your commitment to bringing a practical understanding of prophecy and revelation together will enable others to find and grow in God's best purpose for their lives.

> *Pastor J. Lancaster,*
> *Thomasville, Ga.*

After reading the section entitled " Mystery of Triune Prophecy," I was truly convinced this commentary had something unique to offer. This is possibly the best explanation on the judgments I've read.

> *Pastor R..E. Green,*
> *Los Angeles, Ca.*

1

DEDICATION

This labor of love is first fruits to the giver of life, my Lord and Savior Jesus Christ.

This work is dedicated to the working pastor. The faithful servant, who holds down a job, maintains a marriage, leads a family and feed's the flock of God. The Heavenly Father knows you don't always have the time to do the research you desire. I believe He's recruited me to lend a hand. May the contents of this book become a useful tool for your ministry. Always remember His grace is sufficient.

Special Thanks

To all my friends who assisted in the making of this publication. To Gail and Shirley my grammar queens. To Reggie G. a friend in hard times. To my nephew, the Author whom I find a great inspiration, and a very special thanks to my wife and kids, my greatest supporters and cheerleaders.

PRECEPT
UPON
PRECEPT

COMMENTARY
ON THE BOOK OF
REVELATION AND BIBLE
PROPHECY

LARGE PRINT

By Virgil Thomas

TABLE OF CONTENTS

4

PART 3. MAJOR CHARACTERS pg.53

PART 4. PUTTING IT ALL TOGETHER pg 103

Story written in scripture connecting events and characters not covered in previous material. .(A STORY YOU DON'T WANT TO MISS !)

INTRODUCTION

THE WONDERS OF PROPHECY

Prophecy is fascinating .To have something spoken before it happens and to see it come to pass is a reminder of how finite we are. It also speaks of dimensions that we as human beings have yet to enter. There will always be a curiosity with what could and can be. God designed us this way.

There was a man named Simeon, Luke ch 2 v 25. This man was waiting to see prophecy fulfilled in his time -- the coming of the Savior and the consultation of Israel. Daniel the prophet, in Dan 9v25, recorded that from the command to rebuild Jerusalem to messiah the prince would be 69 weeks or weeks of years (483 yrs). The command came in (Nehemiah 2 v 5) *"And I said unto the king, if it please the king, and if thy servant found favor in thy sight, that thou wouldest send me unto Judah, unto the city of my fathers' sepulchres, that I may rebuild it. "* The year Nehemiah tells us (ch.2:1) *"And it came to pass in the month in the twentieth year of Ar-ta-xerx-es the king, that wine was before him: and I took it up to the king. Now I had not been beforetime sad in his presence. "* Historians date this (Sir Robert Anderson) (Astronomer Royal) 14th March 445 B.C. 483 years (at 360 days) from this date is April 6th 29 B.C. (Matthew 21:4 - 9) *" All this was done, that it might be fulfilled which was spoken by the prophet, saying, Tell ye the daughter of Si-on, Behold, thy King cometh unto thee, meek, and sitting upon an ass, and a colt the foal of an ass. And the disciples went, and did as Jesus commanded them, and bought the ass, and the colt, and put on them their clothes, and they set him thereon. And a very great multitude spread their garments in the way; others cut down branches from the trees, and strewed them in the way. And the multitudes that went before, and that followed, cried saying, Hosanna to the son of David: Blessed is he that cometh in the name of the Lord; Hosanna in the highest. "* The day Jesus declared Himself Messiah! (Date Ref. Josephus)

Though the scripture revealed the coming of Christ to set up His Kingdom, there is nothing indicating date of birth nor the age he would be when he came unto His own. The scriptures do reveal the season & events that would surround it. The word of God declares it is the glory of God to conceal a thing. God revealed to this man and a woman named Anna truth that has been a mystery since the foundations of the world. Paul says (1 Corinthians 15:51-52) *"Behold, I shew you a mystery; We shall not all sleep, but we shall all be changed, In a moment, in the twinkling if an eye, at the last trump: for the trumpet shall sound, and the dead shall be raised incorruptible, and we shall be changed."* God has given us prophecy so like Simeon and Anna we may <u>rejoice with anticipation,</u> <u>know the season</u> and <u>recognize the time.</u>

PART 1.
TOOLS FOR
THE
INTERPRETER

Before you work on an engine its good to know how the parts work.. (Prov.2:1-9)

QUESTIONS TO PONDER.

1. Does God purposely hide truth? If so how is it uncovered?
2. How can I know something spoken in the Old Testament applies today?
3. What does it mean when the bible declares Prophecy is of no private interpretation?

1
BASIC TOOLS / **THE CODE BREAKERS**

(Mark 4:11) "And he said unto them, Unto you it is given to know the mystery of the kingdom of god: but unto them that are without, all these things are done in parables

(Luke 10:21) "In the hour that Jesus rejoiced in spirit, and said, I thank thee, O Father, Lord of heaven and earth, that thou hast hid these things from the wise and prudent, and hast revealed them unto babes: even so, Father; for so it seemed good in thy sight

Only a select few were able to recognize the prophecy of Christ's birth. For generations many Hebrew's have never recognized, " Messiah shall be cut off" (die) Dan 9:26 "But not for himself," for others He would die. As we head into a new century, much is being written on the subject of prophecy. Every time a crisis occurs someone ties it into prophecy. The most common mistakes made by code breakers of old occur because men make prophecy fit their time period. In other words, men jump from biblical truth to assumptions that seem logical with the present world events or conditions. The fall of the Berlin Wall, the development of nuclear weapons by underdeveloped nations and the strengthening of the American economy have proven many of these predictions inaccurate. Though not all these writers are in gross error, much misdirection has come to the body of Christ. People have either been turned off or made fearful. This is sad because God has not spoken these things (end time prophesy) to be ignored. God has spoken these things for our joy and hope.

In this study I want to look at prophecy concerning the last generation. I seek to make no predictions. Instead I want to lay out tools and principles for decoding and let's see as we study what God reveals to you. I believe not only will God give many of you understanding of future events, but strengthen you in the area of doctrine as well. I believe God may also reveal to some of you aspects of prophecy that many don't talk about. Let's begin.

BASIC TOOLS
(Dan. 9:22) "And he informed me, and talked with me, and said, O Daniel I am now come forth to give thee skill and understanding."

Understanding symbols is important. Symbols are used throughout the word of God. Lamp or light for example is a symbol of God's word. You'll find this consistent in both New and Old Testament.

(Psm. 119:105) " Thy **word is a lamp** unto my feet and a light unto my path."
(Prov. 6:23) "For **the commandment is a lamp; and the law is light**; and reproof of instruction are the way of life"

2 Tim 1:10 But is now made manifest by the appearing of our Saviour Jesus Christ, who hath abolished death, and hath brought life and immortality to **light through the gospel**:
2 Cor 4:6 For God, who commanded the light to shine out of darkness, hath shined in our hearts, to give **the light of the knowledge** of the glory of God in the face of Jesus Christ.

This is the test of a symbol! It's meaning must be consistent throughout the New and Old Testament.

Another common mistake in prophecy is to take a symbol in one place and give it a new meaning in another place. *2 Pet 1:20 Knowing this first, that no prophecy of the scripture is of any private interpretation.* This means that all truth can be confirmed by a witness in the scriptures. Neither a doctrine nor revelation can be supported by one verse. Nor does it flip flop in meaning. Example: The beast mentioned throughout the book of Daniel is always symbolic of a ruling king and kingdom. (Empire)

(Dan 7:23-24) " Thus he said, The fourth beast shall be the fourth kingdom upon earth, which shall be diverse from all kingdoms, and shall devour the whole earth, and shall tread it down, and break it in pieces." :24 "And the ten horns out of this kingdom are ten kings that shall arise: and another shall rise after them; and he shall be diverse from the first, and he shall subdue three kings."

Yet many look at the beasts of Revelation ch.13 as just individuals. Remember all symbols are consistent throughout scripture. God is not the author of confusion. If there's a slight change in a symbol's meaning, He'll let us know. Look at as many references as possible on a particular symbol and note their figurative meanings. Example: "the horns" symbolizes kings of a kingdom.

(Dan. 8:20) "The ram which thou sawest having two horns are the kings of Media and Persia......:22 "Now that being broken, whereas four stood up for it, four kingdoms shall stand up out of the nation, but not in his power."
(Zech 1:19 & 21) "And I said unto the angel that talked with me, What be these? And he answered me, These are the horns which have been scattered in Judah, Israel, and Jerusalem.": 21 "Then said I, What come these to do? and he spake, saying, These are the horns which have scattered Judah, so that no man did lift up his head: but these are come to fray them to cast out the horns of the Gentiles, which lifted up their horn over the land of Judah to scatter it."

Look at the consistency in the New Testament.

Rev 17:12 And the ten horns which thou sawest are ten kings, which have received no kingdom as yet; but receive power as kings one hour with the beast.

(Rev. 17:13&16) v.13 "These have one mind, and shall give their power and strength unto the beast.......(v: 16) "And the ten horns which thou sawest upon the beast, these shall hate the whore, and shall make her desolate and naked, and shall eat her flesh, and burn her with fire."

The horns take on a little different meaning and the word explains. Note text: "which have received no kingdom as yet." We will use this tool often!

Another tool is **biblical calculation**. How many days are in a prophetic year, or what frame of time is a symbol? Dan 9:27 mentions a break in middle of week = 3 ½. Rev. 11:2 reveals the same event at 42 months = 3 ½ yrs. Another example: Dan. 7:25 time & times & half time = how long? Note: This is the war against saints during the end time. Rev 13:5-7 forty-two mths. Also communicates in prophetic terms a year equals 360 days.

Always remember words have **figurative or literal meaning.** Check the text to see if it's symbolic or literal. That will be your clue. Here's an example.

(Psm. 110:6) Heads symbolize leaders. (Gen. 43:28) Literally a human head. (Luke 3:16) What is fire here literal or figurative? How about Acts 28:2-3? (Fire =Power & Purging)

Finally -- reading in context. This means look at a verse in light of what is being said as a whole. Example (Mth Ch 6:6), this verse alone could cause you to believe you should only pray alone. The text in Ch.6 begins with the motive of being seen of men. There are other scriptures that show joint and corporate prayer. Mth.26:38, Acts 1:24.

Also we must remember the same God who inspired the Old Testament inspired the New Testament and both will be consistent.

15

2
BREAKS IN TIME.

There is another truth that will help your understanding. It's called a break in time. This is when scripture will speak of one era and in the next sentence speak of another era with gaps of years between. Example…

(Acts 2:16-20 KJV) But this is that which was spoken by the prophet Joel; {17} And it shall come to pass in the last days, saith God, I will pour out of my Spirit upon all flesh: and your sons and your daughters shall prophesy, and your young men shall see visions, and your old men shall dream dreams: {18} And on my servants and on my handmaidens I will pour out in those days of my Spirit; and they shall prophesy:

This is a prophecy of the outpouring of the Holy Ghost. Now observe the next verse. *{19} And I will show wonders in heaven above, and signs in the earth beneath; blood, and fire, and vapour of smoke: {20} The sun shall be turned into darkness, and the moon into blood, before that great and notable day of the Lord come:*

We see here a prophecy of the Day of the Lord, which has not been fulfilled. Another example…

Isa 11:1 And there shall come forth a rod out of the stem of Jesse, and a **branch shall grow out of his roots**::2 And the spirit of the LORD shall rest upon him, the spirit of wisdom and understanding, the spirit of counsel and might, the spirit of knowledge and of the fear of the LORD;

This is a messianic prophecy speaking of a branch from the roots of Jesse, the father of David. This prophecy goes from Jesse's time to that of Jesus Christ. (Rev22v16) **Break in time**. In Dan 11:6-7, the text goes from the time of ancient Greece to the branch of her roots. Which is the last day's prophecy of the beast. This is the same wording as Isa11v1-2. More examples Dan9v26-27,Isa 61v2.

3
THE MASTER KEY JESUS

Rev 19:10 ....: worship God: for the testimony of Jesus is the spirit of prophecy.

"And as he sat upon the Mount of Olives, the disciples came unto him privately, saying Tell us, when shall these things be? What shall be the sign of thy coming, and of the end of the world?" Math 24v3

There are many pieces of prophecy in the word of God. To understand how the pieces fit, we need help. Jesus did not leave us in the dark. Like a map key Jesus is the key to End Time Prophecy. This is a good picture of Mth. Ch 24. Through the words in this chapter many of the pieces are put in order.

The Disciples ask three questions (v3)
1st When shall these things be? **2nd** Sign of your coming? **3rd** Sign of the end? Jesus answers these questions starting with the last to the first. The word "world" is not in the Greek. The proper translation is <u>End of Age.</u>
The **word sign** means mark or indication, miracle or wonder. Mth. 26:48 Judas kiss (indicating act), Mth. 12:38-40 Jonah (Resurrection was the sign) Isaiah 7:14 (Virgin birth) 1Corth. 14:22 (Tongues) <u>Mark</u> 16:17, Isaiah 28:11. Note also as we study Christ's answers to these questions, keep in mind that this discussion with Jesus is only recorded in "Mathew, Mark, and Luke." They record most of the conversation but some fill in the blanks that the others missed. I believe the Holy Spirit has given us the complete picture of what God wanted us to see. **Jesus begins with the last question first.** The pattern we find

in Math.24 will be consistent with other accounts Mk13v1-37 & Lk21.

MATH.CHPT.24

3rd Question: Sign of the end. v4-26. Jesus places them in **two categories.** The Beginning of Sorrows (v4-8) and the Great Tribulation. (v9-26)

2nd Question: Sign of your coming. (v27-31)

1st Question: When shall these things be. (Destruction of the temple) This question is only answered by Luke. Lk21v12-21

WALK THROUGH ANSWERS

THE THIRD QUESTION …The End of The World.

Beginning of sorrows verse 4-8. Signs that show the end is near, not the end but signs that tell us the end is near. End of what? The Age. The end should excite us, not bring an atmosphere of doom to the saint. End of trials, Math. 10:22, end of wicked people, Math. 13:49, work on earth is completed, Math. 24:14, the end of death, 1Corth. 15:24-26, His coming, 1Corth 15:21-24, our reward, Rev. 22:12, Rev. 2:26. The "End" in the Greek is the word Tellos; meaning conclusion, arrive to a point, Termination of a purpose. In John 19:13 the word finished is the same word tellos.

The beginning of sorrow are signs.*First false Christ. The Greek word for Christ is Messiah, meaning "Anointed one of God." He was the look for liberator. Jesus said there would be many. *Wars & rumors of wars. * 3rd Nation against nation, and kingdom against kingdom. (Actual Greek reads race against race and royal ruler against royal ruler) Finally famine, disease and earthquakes. "Note" what we must understand is any or several of these signs can be found through out history. Jesus says you will see all these at work at one time in history. The word sorrows is the Greek word Odin -- it means pang of childbirth. Jesus informs us these are the first pains. These sorrows are consistent with Daniel chpt.11.Before the abomination that makes desolate we see several major conflicts (wars) spanning no less than five years. Dan11v8-29. These involve large nations such as king of the south, (nations of the middle east) kingdom of the beast and his allies, a massive army from the east and north as well as Israel. Math.24v9 Jesus begins the signs of the Great Tribulation

(Mat 24:8-9 KJV) All these *are* the beginning of sorrows. *{9}* Then shall they deliver you up to be afflicted, and shall kill you: and ye shall be hated of all nations for my name's sake.

Notice the word "then". Sorrows are no longer mentioned after this point. The next set of signs we see in the Great Tribulation: individuals murdered for the name of Christ on a global scale, betrayal, false prophets, lawlessness and (while all this is taking place) a gospel witness to the world, then the end. Dan11v33-35 Rev13v4, 7, 14-15, Rev14v3-6. Jesus shows us the marking sign in verse 15.

THE ABOMINATION OF DESOLATION spoken by Daniel. (Dan9v25-27.) Daniel is given revelation concerning Jewish destiny.

(Dan 9:24 KJV) Seventy weeks are determined upon thy people and upon thy holy city, to finish the transgression, and to make an end of sins, and to make reconciliation for iniquity, and to bring in everlasting righteousness, and to seal up the vision and prophecy, and to anoint the most Holy.

These are interpreted **sabbatical weeks**

19

(Lev 25:8 KJV) And thou shalt number seven sabbaths of years unto thee, seven times seven years; and the space of the seven sabbaths of years shall be unto thee forty and nine years.

This method is confirmed, (Rev13v5, Rev11v2-3). Jesus says the abomination, which happens in the middle of the final seven years, marks this Great Tribulation. The Apostle Paul comments on this.

(2 Th 2:3-4 KJV) Let no man deceive you by any means: for *that day shall not come,* except there come a falling away first, and that man of sin be revealed, the son of perdition; *{4}* Who opposeth and exalteth himself above all that is called God, or that is worshipped; so that he as God sitteth in the temple of God, showing himself that he is God.

This marks a time when the Jewish Temple is defiled by the Antichrist.

THE SECOND QUESTION is answered in Math24v27-31.This is call the Second Coming which we cover in detail later.

THE FIRST QUESTION ……When shall these things be? The disciples are referring to the destruction of the Hebrew Temple. Luke 21 is the only place we find the answer to "When shall these things be?" Luke21v12 says, Before any signs of sorrow or end (which signs are mentioned in v11) this must happen, verse 13-24 speaks of persecution of the early church and destruction of the temple. Verse 12 is revealed in *Acts 5:40, Acts 16:37, Acts 7:58-59.* Acts 7 we see the wisdom God poured upon Stephen when brought before the council and he was murdered because of it. Verse 20 speaks of armies. Historians tell us Rome surrounded and destroyed the Jewish temple and Jerusalem 70A.D. They pulled the temple apart stone by stone for the precious gold in which it was overlaid. The warning in verse 21 is for any one in the country to flee and for others not to come near.

What has frustrated decoders of the past is that the language of Matthew and Mark sounds familiar to Luke. Example "Those in Judea flee to mountains," "Desolation's," "woes to pregnant." Yet upon close observation you will notice the difference. Math.24:15 says when you see the <u>abomination of desolation</u>. Luke 21:20, when you see armies around <u>Jerusalem</u> desolation's at hand. Math. 24:21 and Mk.13:19, speaks of worldwide tribulation. Luke 21:23, speaks of wrath and distress of this people (Israel). You will find that of all the gospels, Luke centers more upon the Jewish nation.

The biggest clue is from the Holy Spirit. Mth.24:15 and Mk.13:14 both say (Let him who readeth understand) because this is for future generations. Luke is for that generation and those words are not found.

Note to the student of the word.
The reason you are reading this material is because of a desire to understand. God Himself has planted this seed in you. We have covered the basics, yet I believe this will be the most important lesson for the interpreter.
Most of what's understood in the scriptures is a revelation from God. Unless God opens our eyes the most obvious truth will remain hidden and you'll find yourself with more headaches than answers.
Understanding and revelation are a gift of God. Job 32:8
The word of God declares …

Psa.111:10 The fear of the LORD is the beginning of wisdom: a good understanding have all they that do his commandments: his praise endureth for ever.
Psa.119:99 I have more understanding than all my teachers: for thy testimonies are my meditation. (v:100) I understand more than the ancients, because I keep thy precepts.

Interpretation requires diligence and a heart of obedience. Human pride must die and we must be willing to follow the word even if it travels a path cross grain to our traditional understanding. The Pharisees in the New Testament were blinded from the truth Christ revealed. Their hearts were not set to learn but to validate their own decisions. Obedience to truth was not their motivation, justification of their lifestyle was. Self-righteous pride is the greatest resistor of truth and a gateway to error. Humility is the greatest asset to the student of God's word. Be sure to pray and seek God as you encounter questions along your journey for understanding.

PART 2.
MAJOR EVENTS

When walking through the forest its important to
see where you are stepping.(Math 13:44)

QUESTIONS TO PONDER.

1. How will Gods Justice and Mercy be
    revealed in the Earth?
2. What is the difference between Jewish
    destiny and that of the Church?
3. How many resurrections are there and
    where do they take place?
4. Where is our final destiny? Heaven on
    earth or a place in the heavens?

4
THE DAYS OF VENGEANCE

Lk21:22 speaks of the days of vengeance that prophecy might be fulfilled. We see God's prophecy of judgment foretold in Jerm 6:6-8,upon Israel. Yet the bible speaks about another for the persecutors of his people. Isa.34v4-8, ch63.v3-6 and Jerm46v10. LOOK AT WHAT JESUS SAYS ABOUT THIS ISSUE.

(Isa 61:1-2 KJV) The spirit of the Lord GOD is upon me; because the LORD hath anointed me to preach good tidings unto the meek; he hath sent me to bind up the brokenhearted, to proclaim liberty to the captives, and the opening of the prison to them that are bound; {2} To proclaim the acceptable year of the LORD, and the day of vengeance of our God; to comfort all that mourn;

(Luke 4:18-21 KJV) The Spirit of the Lord is upon me, because he hath anointed me to preach the gospel to the poor; he hath sent me to heal the brokenhearted, to preach deliverance to the captives, and recovering of sight to the blind, to set at liberty them that are bruised, {19} To preach the acceptable year of the Lord. {20} And he closed the book, and he gave it again to the minister, and sat down. And the eyes of all them that were in the synagogue were fastened on him. {21} And he began to say unto them, This day is this scripture fulfilled in your ears.

Why did Jesus close the book when he came to the Day of vengeance? The key is verse 21 "This Day." This was their time for redemption. The Jew first then the Gentile. (also Heb10:30-31) The day of redemption for Israel passed and vengeance came. (Jerm 6:4-8) Now is the Gentile world's time for redemption, the Church era. This too shall pass. (2These. 1:7-8)

THE DAY OF VENGEANCE IN THE LAST DAYS

(Zec 14:4-5 KJV) And his feet shall stand in that day upon the mount of Olives, which is before Jerusalem on the east, and the mount of Olives shall cleave in the midst thereof toward the east and toward the west, and there shall be a very great valley; and half of the mountain shall remove toward the north, and half of it toward the south. {5} And ye shall flee to the valley of the mountains; for the valley of the mountains shall reach unto Azal: yea, ye shall flee, like as ye fled from before the earthquake in the days of Uzziah (king of Judah: and the LORD my God shall come, and all the saints with thee.

Notice this text is very literal and Jesus shall stand on the Mount of Olives, then the return. This could be what the angel referred to in Acts1:11.

Mat 24:27-28 KJV) For as the lightning cometh out of the east, and shineth even unto the west; so shall also the coming of the Son of man be. {28} For wheresoever the carcass is, there will the eagles be gathered together.

Note the words, "cometh out of the east".
Before resurrection of tribulation saints we find this event.

(Rev 7:2 KJV) And I saw another angel ascending from the east, having the seal of the living God: and he cried with a loud voice to the four angels, to whom it was given to hurt the earth and the sea,

The carcasses are the judged armies of the world. God has stopped the mad destruction of sinful mankind. Math24:28, Rev11:18.

(Rev 6:12-15 KJV) And I beheld when he had opened the sixth seal, and, lo, there was a great earthquake; and the sun became black as sackcloth of hair, and the moon became as blood; {13} And the stars of heaven fell unto the earth, even as a fig tree casteth her untimely figs, when she is shaken of a mighty wind. {14} And the heaven departed as a scroll when it is rolled together; and every mountain and island were moved out of their places. {15} And the kings of the earth, and the great men, and the rich men, and the chief captains, and the mighty men, and every bondman, and every free man, hid themselves in the dens and in the rocks of the mountains;

After the Mount of Olives split, a sign will come as a forerunner, then as lightning from the east He will come!

Jesus the spirit of prophecy reveals that the battle has ended on his return. Men are hiding in rocks. The final blow is to be made -- the final judgment. The armies of the world have been destroyed. The four winds are held while the servants of God are sealed. (Rev7:3)The elect are gathered, the judgment poured. Fire and hail falls on the earth. It is done.

(Mat 24:29-31 KJV) Immediately after the tribulation of those days shall the sun be darkened, and the moon shall not give her light, and the stars shall fall from heaven, and the powers of the heavens shall be shaken: {30} And then shall appear the sign of the Son of man in heaven: and then shall all the tribes of the earth mourn, and they shall see the Son of man coming in the clouds of heaven with power and great glory. {31} And he shall send his angels with a great sound of a trumpet, and they shall gather together his elect from the four winds, from one end of heaven to the other.

TIMES OF THE GENTILES Lk21:24-25. We find a break in time in Luke. The text begins with Jerusalem being trampled and Jews being lead into all nations, to the signs of tribulation and second coming. Paul reveals this...

(Rom 11:25 KJV) For I would not, brethren, that ye should be ignorant of this mystery, lest ye should be wise in your own conceits; that blindness in part is happened to Israel, until the fullness of the Gentiles be come in.

Gal3:14, Eph2:11-13 & Eph3:5-6 speaks about all nations'

access to the covenant promise of Abraham and David through the Gospel of Jesus Christ -- the mystery called the church in the New Covenant. *Jerm31:31-34, Heb12:23-24, Jn1:29, Jn3:16, Heb8:13*.

THE TWO ABOMINATIONS

The Abomination of Desolation.

(Dan. 8:9-13) "And out of one of them came forth a little horn, which waxed exceeding great, toward the south, and toward the east, and toward the pleasant land. And it waxed great, even to the host of heaven; and it cast down some of the host and of the stars to the ground, and stamped upon them. Yes, he magnified himself even to the prince of the host, and by him the daily sacrifice was taken away, and the place of his sanctuary was cast down. And an host was given him against the daily sacrifice by reason of transgression, and it cast down the truth to the ground; and it practiced, and prospered. Then I heard one saint speaking, and another saint said unto that certain saint which spake, How long shall be the vision concerning the daily sacrifice, and the transgression of desolation, to give both the sanctuary and the host to be trodden under foot?"

(Dan. 11:31) "And arms shall stand on his part, and they shall pollute the sanctuary of strength, and shall take away the daily sacrifice, and the shall place the abomination that maketh desolate."

This issue has caused some confusion on the placement of the church's resurrection in light of the tribulation. Some believe in post-resurrection of the church and are called Post-tribulationists. (After the tribulation). Pre-tribulationists and Mid-tribulationists believe the church is resurrected before the wrath.(differ in when it starts) Post-tribulationists believe the saints will go through the Great Tribulation. One reason is they don't realize there are two desolations mentioned -- Dan. 8:9-15 & Dan. 11:31-32. They

27

believe the desolation spoken by Jesus has passed. The way to tell the difference is Dan. 8:14-15 & 12:11.

Chpt. 8:14-15 talks about host trodden under and cleansing of sanctuary. A period of 2300 days which equals 6yrs 140 days. Chapter11 & 12 doesn't speak of cleansing sanctuary. It speaks of daily sacrifices taken away plus an abomination set up for 3 ½yrs. There are two desolations in Daniel.

Most Post-tribulationists point to a 6 yr. period of desolation and believe this is the one Jesus is referring to. **Antiochus Iv.** called Epiphanes (Illustrious) who assaulted Jerusalem stop Judaism and set up the worship of Greek gods. 170 to 163 B.C. [Cowels volume library (1933) dates 170 B.C. first assault and his death 163 B.C. Temple was purified 165 B.C. He died of unknown causes.] This fits the first desolation because Antiochus was king of Syria.

Syria is one of four horns that came from the Greek Empire of Alexander the Great (The Little Horn of Dan 8v7-11). Antiochus was one of Syria's latter kings before the Roman empires rise. He was broken without Human Hands, term used in Job34:20 meaning death by natural causes. Always remember the key JESUS. Mth 24:15,21 Dan.12:11. The desolation Jesus quotes is this of Daniel 12 and has not come. Antichus was dead over 193 yrs. when Jesus spoke this. Why would He speak of a desolation to come that has passed?

5
THE RESURRECTIONS

ORDER OF RESURRECTIONS / RAPTURE OF THE CHURCH

What we call the rapture can be best understood as part of the resurrections. There are two resurrections. The rapture of the church is part of the 1st Resurrection.

(1 Cor 15:23 KJV) But every man in his own order: Christ the first fruits; afterward they that are Christ's at his coming.

The Greek word for <u>order</u> here is tagma. It's defined: Orderly in arrangement, a series or succession. The 1st resurrection is not one resurrection but is comprised of several. Jesus is the first. *(1Corth15v23)* and we see others *(Math 24v29-31)*, end of Trib. *(Isa26v19, Job14v13-14, Rev 11v12 1st Thes4v16-17.Dan12v1-2)*
The 2nd resurrection are those whom the 2nd death will have an effect and takes place after 1,000 year reign at The Great White Throne judgment.

(Rev 20:5-6 KJV) But the rest of the dead lived not again until the thousand years were finished. This *is* the first resurrection. *{6}* Blessed and holy *is* he that hath part in the first resurrection: on such the second death hath no power, but they shall be priests of God and of Christ, and shall reign with him a thousand years.

The resurrections are initiated by the voice of Christ. (John5v28-29, Rev.4v1& Rev.11v12).
Notice 1Thess.4v16-17. The Lord descends with the voice/trumpet and saints come to him. The Arch Angel Michael is mentioned five times in scripture, three are related to resurrections Dan12v1-2 Rev.12v7-12

1st resurrection includes all those who have received Jesus Christ as savior before 1,000 years. The rapture of church, Old Testament saints, taking up of witnesses, rapture of the elect, (Jesus being 1st fruits) are all part of 1st Resurrection. I Thess. 4;16-17 speaks purely of Christian resurrection. This is not the return but the meeting in the air. Yet Jesus speaks of a resurrection in John 5:28-29 that is saved and unsaved at His coming. (Dan12v2, Rev.14v14-20) One resurrection is unto life and the other unto death. Matthew 24:29-31 is often mistaken for rapture of church.

(Mat 24:29-31 KJV) Immediately after the tribulation of those days shall the sun be darkened, and the moon shall not give her light, and the stars shall fall from heaven, and the powers of the heavens shall be shaken: {30} And then shall appear the sign of the Son of man in heaven: and then shall all the tribes of the earth mourn, and they shall see the Son of man coming in the clouds of heaven with power and great glory. {31} And he shall send his angels with a great sound of a trumpet, and they shall gather together his elect from the four winds, from one end of heaven to the other.

This is the rapture of Gods Elect at the second coming. Rev. 7:9-14 At this rapture, Christ will come with His saints. (I Thess.3:13, Zech. 14:1&5. Rev.1v7, Dan7v13, Rev.19v11-20) This clearly follows the Tribulation.

_ (Rev 19:11-15 KJV) And I saw heaven opened, and behold a white horse; and he that sat upon him *was* called Faithful and True, and in righteousness he doth judge and make war. {12} His eyes *were* as a flame of fire, and on his head *were* many crowns; and he had a name written, that no man knew, but he himself. {13} And he *was* clothed with a vesture dipped in blood: and his name is called The Word of God {14} And the armies *which were* in heaven followed him upon white horses, clothed in fine linen, white and clean. {15} And out of his mouth goeth a sharp sword, that with it he should smite the nations: and he shall rule them with a rod of iron: and he treadeth the winepress of the fierceness and wrath of Almighty God.

(Joel 2:10-11 KJV) The earth shall quake before them; the heavens shall tremble: the sun and the moon shall be dark, and the stars shall withdraw their shining: {11} And the LORD shall utter his voice before his army: for his camp *is* very great: for *he is* strong that executeth his word: for the day of the LORD *is* great and very terrible; and who can abide it?

John makes it clear that God is about to smite the nations *(Day of the Lord)* and the saints are with Him. This ends the Tribulation, which Jesus marks as the time of gathering His elect.

It's important to observe the nature of God through the scriptures. **God delivers his people from wrath**. That is what we see in I Thess. 4:16-18 . Rev.3 :10.

(Rev 3:10 KJV) Because thou hast kept the word of my patience, I also will keep thee from the hour of temptation, which shall come upon all the world, to try them that dwell upon the earth.

In this prophetic verse the word temptation has the same meaning as the Hebrew word used in Deut.ch4:34 describing Gods judgment on Egypt.

(Deu 4:34 KJV) Or hath God assayed to go *and* take him a nation from the midst of *another* nation, by temptations, by signs, and by wonders, and by war, and by a mighty hand, and by a stretched out arm, and by great terrors, according to all that the LORD your God did for you in Egypt before your eyes?

Jesus gives us **two Old Testament illustration.**
Noah and Lot. (Mth.24:36-39, Luke 17:28-29) Both were out of harms way before the wrath of God began. The time frame in these illustrations for deliverance and wrath are very close.

(2 Pet 2:4-9 KJV) For if God spared not the angels that sinned, but cast *them* down to hell, and delivered *them* into chains of darkness, to be reserved unto judgment; *{5}* And spared not the old world, but saved Noah the eighth *person,* a preacher of righteousness, bringing in the flood upon the world of the ungodly; *{6}* And turning the cities of Sodom and Gomorrha into ashes condemned *them* with an overthrow, making *them* an ensample unto those that after should live ungodly; *{7}* And delivered just Lot, vexed with the filthy conversation of the wicked: *{8}* (For that righteous man dwelling among them, in seeing and hearing, vexed *his* righteous soul from day to day with *their* unlawful deeds;) *{9}* The Lord knoweth how to deliver the godly out of temptations, and to reserve the unjust unto the day of judgment to be punished:

JESUS DOESN'T COME LIKE A THIEF FOR THE CHURCH

The term "come like a thief" always refers to a time during the tribulation period. The term "**appearing or Christ appearing**" refers to the resurrection of the church prior to the tribulation period.
This is a time of rewards and judgments for the believers in Jesus Christ sometimes called the judgment seat of Christ.

(1 Pet 1:7 KJV) That the trial of your faith, being much more precious than of gold that perisheth, though it be tried with fire, might be found unto praise and honour and glory at the appearing of Jesus Christ:

(1 Pet 5:4 KJV) And when the chief Shepherd shall appear, ye shall receive a crown of glory that fadeth not away.

We see saints with crowns before the wrath begins. Rev4v4-10

(2 Pet 3:10 KJV) But the day of the Lord will come as a thief in the night; in the which the heavens shall pass away with a great noise, and the elements shall melt with fervent heat, the earth also and the works that are therein shall be burned up.

Another example

(1 Th 5:2-3 KJV) For yourselves know perfectly that the day of the Lord so cometh as a thief in the night. {3} For when they shall say, Peace and safety; then sudden destruction cometh upon them, as travail upon a woman with child; and they shall not escape.
(Also 1 Th 1:9-10 KJV, Zep 1:14-15 KJV)

The issue of wrath is important to see. Verse 9 of 1st Thess.5 Paul assures the saints God has not appointed them to wrath. (Also Rm2v5-10) The warning in Rev16v15 "Behold I come as a thief" comes in context of Armageddon in which the Day of Lord takes place.
We find the **Appearing** a special time of judgment before the "White throne Judgment" Notice also the Judgment of saints before that of the world.

(2Tim 4:1 KJV) I charge *thee* therefore before God, and the Lord Jesus Christ, who shall judge the quick and the dead at **his appearing and his kingdom;** Notice two judgments are being listed here.

(Rom 14:10-12 KJV) But why dost thou judge thy brother? or why dost thou set at naught thy brother? for we shall all stand before the judgment seat of Christ. {11} For it is written, *As* I live, saith the Lord, every knee shall bow to me, and every tongue shall confess to God. {12} So then every one of us shall give account of himself to God.

(2 Tim 4:8 KJV) Henceforth there is laid up for me a crown of righteousness, which the Lord, the righteous judge, shall give me at that day: and not to me only, but unto all them also that love **his appearing**.
...also 1 Pet.1v7

HEB. 9v 27-28 Speaks also of Christ appearing a second time -- unlike the first **for sin** (work of the cross) but for **salvation** (deliverance from wrath to come).

THE ORDER OF RESSURECTIONS

FIRST RESURRECTION

1. **Jesus** first fruits .   1 Corth 15v23

2. Open graves of saints immediately after Christ's resurrection. Math27v52,53

3.**The Church** and Old test. Saints.Isa26v19-21,Job19v2526
                    1thes4v16, 1Corth15v52,Rev12v7-12

4.**The witnesses** Rev11v12,(note) Paul states 1Corth15v53, we are changed upon resurrection and put on immortality. The witnesses don't arrive as immortals.

5.**Tribulation Martyrs and Unrepentant Dead of the Tribulation**. This is the only dual resurrection mentioned of the dead. It takes place at the end of tribulation, at the Second Coming, Rev14v14-20, Dan12v1-2, Maht24v29-31, John5v28-29, Rev20v4-6. It is also referred to in the parable of wheat and tares and the sheep and goats. See Rev14v9-11&19-20,Rev19v20-21,Isa 34v8-10. After the resurrection of martyrs the unrepentant dead of the tribulation are judged with fire and cast in hell.

THE SECOND RESSURECTION

6.The Great White Throne Judgment.Rev20v12, Rev20v6, Job14v12

6.
THE LAST YEARS OF TIME

Jesus gives us signs that describe the atmosphere of the final years. This is important to us because Dan.ch 9 speaks of seventy weeks of sevens that are determined for his people. God is giving Daniel nformation concerning prophecy for the Hebrew people. God gives ime frames that are initiated by signs. (See intro.) Most interpret this as sabbatical weeks. (Weeks of years) Lev25v8 It's amazing how God gives time frames for these historical events in Jewish history. What's incredible is the **final week** of Jewish destiny *(seven year period)* effect's us all. (Dan.9v24-27) Over seventy percent of the book of Revelation deals with this time chpts.4-20). Yet Jesus is covering more in the Mount of Olives discourse than seven years. He gives **the parable of the Fig tree.**

(Mat 24:32-34 KJV) Now learn a parable of the fig tree; When his branch is yet tender, and putteth forth leaves, ye know that summer *is* nigh: *{33}* So likewise ye, when ye shall see all these things, know that it is near, *even* at the doors. *{34}* Verily I say unto you, this generation shall not pass, till all these things be fulfilled.

The fig tree is a reference to the Jewish people of the Old Testament. Jesus is quoting Song of Sol.2v11-13. This reappearing is believed to mark 1948 statehood of the Jews. I believe winter, as many commentators, describes the period of exile from the land due to disobedience. (Duet.28v63-68) Paul the apostle gives us this insight.

Rom 11:25 For I would not, brethren, that ye should be ignorant of this mystery, est ye should be wise in your own conceits; that blindness in part is happened to Israel, until the fulness of the Gentiles be come in.

Paul declares that God has not abandoned nor completed his dealings with Israel. They are blind until the season of the church is completed. He goes on to say they shall be saved and a deliverer shall come out of Zion, which is literally Jerusalem. The scripture says this reemergence of the fig tree (Israel) and the appearing of the signs mentioned in Math.chpt.24 will mark the final generation before the end. This is in line with the final week of Daniel. Yet it should not be interpreted as the beginning of Daniel's final week .The fig tree is clearly a sign that marks the nearness of this time. My point is there have been many false tribulation alarms. We must be careful not to read prophecy into an event but place the event in prophecy. A common mistake is to force scripture into a belief or belief system. Some commentators have proclaimed the beginning of sorrows is the beginning of seven-year agreement. They assign the Seal Judgments as the first 3 ½ years. The trumpet and vials are the Great Tribulation that begins in the middle.

The problem is this has no scriptural support.
The Sixth Seal shows the world armies destroyed, the earth shattere and a declaration the Day of the Wrath is come. Rev. 6v12-17
It's all over before we get to the middle of the week and there are fifteen judgments left to go. Belief with out scriptural support becomes vague and confusing. The bible says in….

James 3:17 But the wisdom that is from above is first pure, then peaceable, gentle, and easy to be entreated, full of mercy and good fruits, without partiali and without hypocrisy.

The bible says the last seven year period is and agreement made by the prince who shall come *(antichrist)* with Israel. (Dan 9v27).
Halfway in the agreement he breaks it. (Dan 11v31) This triggers the Great Tribulation. Dan12v1. The beginning of sorrows can begin a time before this agreement. We are experiencing all of those signs today! Math24v4-8

7
THE GREAT TRIBULATION

Now lets look at the GREAT TRIBULATION (math.ch24v21)

(Zep 1:14-17 KJV) The great day of the LORD is near, it is near, and hasteth greatly, even the voice of the day of the LORD: the mighty man shall cry there bitterly. {15} That day is a day of wrath, a day of trouble and distress, a day of wasteness and desolation, a day of darkness and gloominess, a day of clouds and thick darkness, {16} A day of the trumpet and alarm against the fenced cities, and against the high towers. {17} And I will bring distress upon men, that they shall walk like blind men, because they have sinned against the LORD: and their blood shall be poured out as dust, and their flesh as the dung.

Lets first identify the Great Tribulation in scripture. There are several names that refer to this time period. Dan12v1Time of trouble, Jerm30v1-11 Jacobs trouble, Isa13v11-14 Wrath of the Lord, Psm110v5-7, Isa63v3-6 Wrath of God and Zeph1v14 Day of the Lord. All speak of worldwide judgment. **They also point to specific events in the Tribulation period.**

NAMES TO KNOW / LAY OUT OF END TIME EVENTS.

BEGINNING OF TRIBULATION
Called the GREAT TRIBULATION, covering not only beginning but the entire3 ½ year period. Math24v21. Also called DAY OF CHRIST   Phil.1v10 , Phil.2v16 and 2These.2v2
WRATH OF GOD
Rev. 15:1-7, Rev.16:1-16 they are the last plagues,7 vials.

THE DAY OF THE LORD

Ezk13v5,Ezk30v3, Joel 2:10-11 ,3v16& 2:31,   Zech..14:1-4,
Zeph. 1:14-17,Jerm6v6-12, Isa13v6-10 ,Amos5v18
This event is always tied in with Armageddon, this is the day of
vengeance.

TIME OF TROUBLE

The execution of the day of the lord. Dan12v1-2, Job38v21-22,
Jer30v7-8,Psm27v4-5, Isa33v2-3,

SECOND COMING OF CHRIST

Referred to as the Second Advent Math16V28,Math24v30-31,
Math25v30-31, 1stCorth1v7-8,1stThess2v19,James5v7-8
The second coming brings a close to Daniels 70th week and the
beginning of the promised kingdom and rule of JESUS CHRIST

WINE PRESS OF HIS WRATH

Rev11v18,, 14v10-11,,14v19,,19v20 also8v5
This is the final judgment

Understanding these terms is of great importance.
The Day of Christ can be mistaken for the Time of Trouble.
Placing events in the right order helps us stay on track.

LAY OUT OF END TIME EVENTS

THE DAY OF CHRIST

The day of Christ is closely related to the Appearing. (see pg 29)
(2 Th 2:1-4 KJV) Now we beseech you, brethren, by **the coming** of our
Lord Jesus Christ, and *by* **our gathering** together unto him, {2} That ye
be not soon shaken in mind, or be troubled, neither by spirit, nor by word,
nor by letter as from us, as that the day of Christ is at hand. {3} Let no
man deceive you by any means: for *that day shall not come,* except there
come a falling away first, and <u>that man of sin be revealed</u>, the son of
perdition; {4} Who opposeth and exalteth himself above all that is called

God, or that is worshipped; so that he as God sitteth in the temple of God, showing himself that he is God.
(2 Th 2:7-8 KJV) For the mystery of iniquity doth already work: only he who now letteth *will let,* until he be taken out of the way. *{8}* And then shall that <u>Wicked be revealed, whom the Lord shall consume with the spirit of his mouth,</u> **and** shall destroy with the brightness of his coming:

Paul deals with two issues here, the "Coming" and the "Gathering." Paul tells us the Day of Christ happens after the man of sin is revealed. This is neither the resurrection of the church nor the Second Coming. The Second Coming of Jesus shows the man of sin defeated. He clearly states here the reveling is the abomination that makes desolate. **Before the man of sin** can be revealed there is the removal, v7-8

Note :(He =Jn.14v17&16v8 ..It is the Spirit at work through the church that resist lawlessness during this time period)

We see the church gathered together before the revealing of the beast Rev12v10 & 13, Rev3v10. Paul states the Day of Christ begins after the abomination. The book of Daniel gives us a glimpse.

(Dan 7:8-9 KJV) I considered the horns, and, behold, there came up among them another little horn, before whom there were three of the first horns plucked up by the roots: and, behold, <u>in this horn *were* eyes like the eyes of man, and a mouth speaking great things.</u> *{9}* I beheld till the thrones were cast down, and the Ancient of days did sit, whose garment *was* white as snow, and the hair of his head like the pure wool: his throne *was like* the fiery flame, *and* his wheels *as* burning fire.

After the horn is revealed then we see thrones cast down (NIV. SET IN PLACE). The picture of Christ In white garments and wool hair (Rev.1v14) is Christ the judge. Note in Rev1v14 the two-edged sword precedes from his mouth. (Psa 149:6-9 KJV) *Let* the high *praises* of God *be* in their mouth, and a two-edged sword in their hand; *{7}* To execute vengeance upon the heathen, *and* punishments upon the people; *{8}* To bind their kings with chains, and their nobles with fetters of iron; *{9}* <u>To execute upon them the judgment written: this honour have all his saints</u>. Praise ye the LORD (.also Heb4v12, 2Thes2v7-8) This Is the Day of Christ.

The Day of Christ begins with the revealing of the beast and opening of the books. The opening of the books or scrolls begins the pronouncements of worldwide judgment. This was the concern of the Thessalonians. They thought they had missed the rapture and the Judgments were about to begin. Paul tells us the Lord will consume the wicked one, two ways. The first was by The Spirit of His Mouth, later with the brightness of His coming.

(Dan 7:10 KJV) A fiery stream issued and came forth from before him: thousand thousands ministered unto him, and ten thousand times ten thousand stood before him: the judgment was set, and the books were opened. Compare with (Rev 4:5 KJV) & (Rev 5:6-8 KJV)

(Rev 5:11-12 KJV) And I beheld, and I heard the voice of many angels round about the throne and the beasts and the elders: and the number of them was ten thousand times ten thousand, and thousands of thousands; *{12}* Saying with a loud voice, Worthy is the Lamb that was slain to receive power, and riches, and wisdom, and strength, and honour, and glory, and blessing.....the beginning of the Great Tribulation.

We see the throne room setting in Daniel also in Rev 4:4 And round about the throne *were* four and twenty seats: and upon the seats I saw four and twenty elders sitting, clothed in white raiment; and they had on their heads crowns of gold.

Note: they've already bowed the knee, confessed and received their crowns. Paul makes clear that the righteous receive judgment first.1Corth3v12-15,1Corth4v5, Rm14v10, 2Corth5v10. (2 Tim 4:1 KJV) I charge *thee* therefore before God, and the Lord Jesus Christ, who shall judge the quick and the dead at his appearing and his kingdom;

The Appearing is the judgment of the saints .The Kingdom is the judgment of the unsaved. The order is the house of God first. (1Pet4v16-17). The appearing shows saints receiving crowns (reward). (2Tim4v8)

In conclusion we see the 1st resurrection (Rapture) brings us to the Appearing (The Judgment of the saints).The Abomination (revealing) begins the Day of Christ. The Lamb of God opening the scrolls of judgment in the presence of His saints begins the Great Tribulation.

THE DAY OF THE LORD

One important truth to understand about the Day of the Lord is that **it is one day**. The day God will take vengeance on the heathen and deliver His people. It's not a particular judgment but a series of judgments. The day of lord begins after 6th vial, and its signs are seen in the 7th seal and Trumpet

(Zec 14:7-9 KJV) But it shall be one day which shall be known to the LORD, not day, nor night: but it shall come to pass, that at evening time it shall be light. {8} And it shall be in that day, that living waters shall go out from Jerusalem; half of them toward the former sea, and half of them toward the hinder sea: in summer and in winter shall it be. {9} And the LORD shall be king over all the earth: in that day shall there be one LORD, and his name one.

This is the day that will bring an end to the battle of Armageddon. The focal point for this day is Jerusalem. The major signs are an earthquake, the sun darkened and the moon turned to blood. The mystery of summer and winter in the same day could be explained Job 38v22-23. The city will be under

41

siege by foreign troops during the battle of Armageddon. There is no time frame for Armageddon. The word for battle is polemos, which signifies warfare or campaign.

(Oba 1:15-17 KJV) For the day of the LORD *is* near upon all the heathen: as thou hast done, it shall be done unto thee: thy reward shall return upon thine own head. *{16}* For as ye have drunk upon my holy mountain, *so* shall all the heathen drink continually, yea, they shall drink, and they shall swallow down, and they shall be as though they had not been. *{17}* But upon mount Zion shall be deliverance, and there shall be holiness; and the house of Jacob shall possess their possessions.

TIME OF TROUBLE

(Isa 33:2-3 KJV) O LORD, be gracious unto us; we have waited for thee: be thou their arm every morning, our salvation also in the time of trouble. *{3}* At the noise of the tumult the people fled; at the lifting up of thyself the nations were scattered.

The prophet cries out for God to be their salvation in time of trouble. He describes God lifting Himself up and the nations being scattered. Zech14v3 puts this in the Day of the Lord. Dan12v1-2 shows this taking place after the beast sets up his palace between the seas and the holy mountain. Jerm30v7-8 proclaims at this time the yoke shall be broken off Israel. This seems to point specifically to the Jews struggle in the Day of the Lord.

THE SECOND COMING OF CHRIST

(Acts 1:11 KJV) Which also said, Ye men of Galilee, why stand ye gazing up into heaven? This same Jesus, which is taken up from you into heaven, shall so come in like manner as ye have seen him go into heaven.

To grasp the second coming we must remember it is **more than one event**. The first coming of Christ involved a series of events, which ended with the establishing of the spiritual kingdom of God. The second is the completion with a physical kingdom on earth.

This is the day Jesus gathers up his elect. Paul tells us after his coming then comes the end, (1st Corth.15v23-24) and then the ushering in of the kingdom. The beast is destroyed by the Brightness of His Coming, (2Thess 2v8) and the ungodly judged. (2Pet3v4-5) 1stThes.2v19 alludes that Paul's joy is that they're in the Lord's presence on that day (possibly as part of the cloud of saints)

The difference between the Second Coming and the Day of the Lord is the Day of the Lord focuses on wrath and Judgment. The Second Coming is about redemption and vindication. (2Thess.2v8, James5v7, 2Pet.1v16)

ARMAGEDDON

(Rev 16:14-16 KJV) For they are the spirits of devils, working miracles, *which* go forth unto the kings of the earth and of the whole world, to gather them to the battle of that great day of God Almighty. *{15}* Behold, I come as a thief. Blessed *is* he that watcheth, and keepeth his garments, lest he walk naked, and they see his shame. *{16}* And he gathered them together into a place called in the Hebrew tongue Armageddon.

THREE PLACES OF BATTLE

Armageddon is the place called Megiddo (place of crowds) on southern rim of Esdraelon plain. This is also a name for the final battles of the tribulation period. Here God judges the nations for their persecution of Israel, (Joel3v2) the blood of the Martyrs, (Rev6v10-11) pride and sin of mankind. Isa.3v9-13.

Armageddon is a focal point for not just one battle but many. These are the battles that usher in the return of Christ. Their locations are the (1) hill or city of Megiddo, (2) Valley of Jehoshaphat, an extended area east of Jerusalem, a deep ravine that separates Jerusalem from Mt of Olives. The ravine is lined on both sides with Jewish and Muslim sepulchers. (3) The Euphrates river. This is the largest river in western Asia. It flows from the Armenian Mts. into the Persian Gulf. **The link we find in prophecy for all three is the Day of the Lord.**

Armageddon
(Isa 13:4-6 KJV) The noise of a multitude in the mountains, like as of a great people; a tumultuous noise of the kingdoms of nations gathered together: the LORD of hosts mustereth the host of the battle. {5} They come from a far country, from the end of heaven, *even* the LORD, and the weapons of his indignation, to destroy the whole land. {6} Howl ye; for the day of the LORD *is* at hand; it shall come as a destruction from the Almighty.

Valley of Jehoshaphat
(Joel 3:12-14 KJV) Let the heathen be wakened, and come up to the valley of Jehoshaphat: for there will I sit to judge all the heathen round about. {13} Put ye in the sickle, for the harvest is ripe: come, get you down; for the press is full, the vats overflow; for their wickedness *is* great. {14} Multitudes, multitudes in the valley of decision: for the day of the LORD *is* near in the valley of decision.

The Euphrates
(Jer 46:10 KJV) For this *is* the day of the Lord GOD of hosts, a day of vengeance, that he may avenge him of his adversaries: and the sword shall devour, and it shall be satiated and made drunk with their blood: for the Lord GOD of hosts hath a sacrifice in the north country by the river Euphrates.

THE ARMIES INVOLVED
The Beast alias King of the North.
(Vile One of Dan ch11). His coalition of two nations know as
The False Prophet , Revch13.and the *Ten horns* Rev.ch17.

King of the South (Nations of Middle east.)

The kings of the East, Rev16v12
Those beyond the Euphrates and various powers of North
Africa are mentioned. The entire world will fall into one of
these camps.

I exclude the prophecies of Gog and Magog in Ezk.38 because I
found no connection to the Day of the Lord prophecies. They
rather point to the Millennium prophecies (Rev 20). They speak
of a time when Israel dwells safely. No one will dwell safely in
the tribulation. The Millennium rebellion seems to be instigated
by Gog and Magog. Ezek.38 account also makes them the
primary focus, for the burial place is named after them. They
are not the primary focus in Armageddon. They will no doubt
be involved in Armageddon and are possibly the threat from the
north in Dan.11v44

THE ORDER OF BATTLE

The Day of the Lord is not the battle of Armageddon. It is an
event that takes place during the final world conflict. The Day
of the Lord is one day! Zech, 14v7

(Joel 2:31 KJV) The sun shall be turned into darkness, and the moon into
blood, before the great and the terrible day of the LORD come.

(Joel 3:14-15 KJV) Multitudes, multitudes in the valley of decision: for the day of the LORD *is* near in the valley of decision. *{15}* The sun and the moon shall be darkened, and the stars shall withdraw their shining.

(Zec 14:2-3 KJV) For I will gather all nations against Jerusalem to battle; and the city shall be taken, and the houses rifled, and the women ravished; and half of the city shall go forth into captivity, and the residue of the people shall not be cut off from the city. *{3}* Then shall the LORD go forth, and fight against those nations, as when he fought in the day of battle.
(Joel 2:31 KJV) The sun shall be turned into darkness, and the moon into blood, before the great and the terrible day of the LORD come.

Joel reveals the sign "moon to blood" is before the Day of the Lord. He also shows us the gathering of troops. Finally we see Zechariah's prophecy revealing the battle going forth into Jerusalem. This is when the Lord goes forth. (See also Joel3v16, Joel2v1-11)
This is the Day of the lord. This marks the return of Christ. This ends the battle of Armageddon - the earthquake being the marker of this event. (Zec.14v4-5, Rev.5v19)

The Wedding Feast

Rev. 19:6-7 To really grasp the meaning here, it's good to do research. For example the Nation of Chittim in the Old Testament is Cyprus. Leaven is a foreign word to many. In a generation of modern supermarkets very few people use yeast or could identify the word without some checking. I know a young man who thought the yoke of Christ revolved around an egg. You may laugh, but most of the word of God is written in the terms of a time and culture unlike our own. You will find our Lord used many Jewish terms concerning weddings. In the time of our Lord, weddings were more a legal affair than today's weddings.

There was the establishing of a price to be paid for the bride. There was the covenant (contract or agreement), sealing contract (sharing the cup), and paying the price (dowry). After this was settled he would depart to prepare the chamber. The marriage was already official but the wedding would not begin until a suitable chamber was prepared. The father of the groom oversaw this. Upon his approval the groom could retrieve his bride and the wedding would begin. In that time period most brides never knew when he would arrive with the best man. They would have clothing packed and lamps ready, because evening was the traditional departure time. The best man would shout and off they'd go. Ref. (Zola Levitt Christian Love Story). The Wedding Feast was seven days, but the bride and groom didn't attend until later in the week. They were in the chamber and evidence must be produced of the bride's virginity. Unfaithfulness was punishable by death. Then they would exit the chamber into celebration with applause. Remember...

(John 14:1-3) Let not your heart be troubled: ye believe in God, believe also in me.:2 In my Father's house are many mansions: if *it were* not *so,* I would have told you. I go to prepare a place for you.:3 And if I go and prepare a place for you, I will come again, and receive you unto myself; that where I am, *there* ye may be also.

(Mat 25:5-9) While the bridegroom tarried, they all slumbered and slept.:6 And at midnight there was a cry made, Behold, the bridegroom cometh; go ye out to meet him.:7 Then all those virgins arose, and trimmed their lamps.:8And the foolish said unto the wise, Give us of your oil; for our lamps are gone out :9 But the wise answered, saying, *Not so;* lest there be not enough for us and you: but go ye rather to them that sell, and buy for yourselves.

Here in Rev. Chapter 19 we see them exiting the chambers. The issue is faithfulness. The bride was faithful -- true to her husband. Followers of Jesus Christ are the Bride and He is the Bridegroom. In John 3:29 Paul makes this comment.

(2 Cor 11:2 KJV) For I am jealous over you with godly jealousy: for I have espoused you to one husband, that I may present *you as* a chaste virgin to Christ.Also Eph. 5:25-26 31-32.

We are espoused to Christ. The necessary requirements have been met. The New Testament, (covenant/contract) in which he became the sacrificial Lamb, was paid in full. The Hebrew word actually means a cutting. For animals were divided and passed through on an agreement. Gensis 15, Jerm 34:18-19. Jesus Christ has given us a covenant of Grace. (Eph 2:8-18 KJV)

The heavenly Father has prepared a wedding feast. Christ has paid the dowry with His blood, the wine of communion. We as the Bride have a responsibility to keep ourselves undefiled by the world. Chaste means innocent and pure.

Rev 3:4 Thou hast a few names even in Sardis which have not defiled their garments; and they shall walk with me in white: for they are worthy.:5 He that overcometh, the same shall be clothed in white raiment; and I will not blot out his name out of the book of life, but I will confess his name before my Father, and before his angels.

Mat 22:11 And when the king came in to see the guests, he saw there a man which had not on a wedding garment::12 And he saith unto him, Friend, how camest thou in hither not having a wedding garment? And he was speechless.:13 Then said the king to the servants, Bind him hand and foot, and take him away, and cast him into outer darkness; there shall be weeping and gnashing of teeth.

The bride awaits the shout, and to be taken away to the place prepared.

THE CHAMBER.

Isaiah the prophet saw a vision of the last days. He was himself being raised from the dead with others. He says he is raised from the dead and enters a chamber. He resides there until the indignations past. The indignation is a term for the tribulation period. This is a perfect picture of I thess.4v16.

Isa 26:19 Thy dead men shall live, together with my dead body shall they arise. Awake and sing, ye that dwell in dust: for thy dew is as the dew of herbs, and the earth shall cast out the dead.:20 Come, my people, enter thou into thy chambers, and shut thy doors about thee: hide thyself as it were for a little moment, until the indignation be overpast.:21 For, behold, the LORD cometh out of his place to punish the inhabitants of the earth for their iniquity: the earth also shall disclose her blood, and shall no more cover her slain.

In chapter 19, the bride and bridegroom enter the feast.

Rev 19:7 Let us be glad and rejoice, and give honour to him: for the marriage of the Lamb is come, and his wife hath made herself ready.:8 And to her was granted that she should be arrayed in fine linen, clean and white: for the fine linen is the righteousness of saints.:9 And he saith unto me, Write, Blessed are they which are called unto the marriage supper of the Lamb. And he saith unto me, These are the true sayings of God. Also Rev 22v16-17

The book of Joel records this moment in end time prophecy.

(Joel 2:15 KJV) Blow the trumpet in Zion, sanctify a fast, call a solemn assembly: (Joel 2:16 KJV) Gather the people, sanctify the congregation, assemble the elders, gather the children, and those that suck the breasts: let the bridegroom go forth of his chamber, and the bride out of her closet.

Blessed are they that are called to supper of the Lamb. What is interesting is the statement made in Rev.19v17-18. Truly this will be a time of celebration for the indignation has passed. In Matthew 24 (after tribulations) the promise has come and the final scene is about to close (Hosea 2:18-19).

8
THE THOUSAND YEAR REIGN (Millennium)

Rev 20:2 And he laid hold on the dragon, that old serpent, which is the Devil, and Satan, and bound him a thousand years,

Rev 20: 5 But the rest of the dead lived not again until the thousand years were finished. This is the first resurrection.:6 Blessed and holy is he that hath part in the first resurrection: on such the second death hath no power, but they shall be priests of God and of Christ, and shall reign with him a thousand years.:7 And when the thousand years are expired, Satan shall be loosed out of his prison,

The Thousand Year Reign is a time of perfect peace and governance under Christ. The proclamation at the end of the tribulation is the kingdoms of this world are now the kingdoms of our God! The world will become a type of Eden where all the sons of Adam can experience life in fellowship with God, unhindered by the serpent. Love towards one another can truly flourish as we rebuild our world under Gods guidance.

Revelation Chpt.20 shows us the perfect order. After the judgment of the world's armies by our Lord, the Devil is bound for the duration of the Millennium. The tribulation saints will reign with Christ during this period, as will all who are part of the first resurrection. (See also 2 Tim 2:12) How we will reign is a bit of a mystery. We do know those that have been resurrected will have glorified bodies and some how dwell and conduct business among those that are human. The tribulation Martyrs will serve in the temple. (Rev 7:14-15) All who were resurrected before the tribulation will Judge the Gentile World. (1Cor 6:2) The Apostles will Judge the Jewish people. (Luke 22:29) The 144,000 will be priest and Levites to God. (Isa.66:19-22)

There will also be a special quality of life. People will live longer. Individuals who reach the age of a hundred will physically be as a child. There will be a harmony in nature that hadn't existed since the Garden of Eden -- where the lion will lie down with the Lamb.

There is also a period of unknown time. Satan is loosed after the Millennium. There is a time period by which nations are corrupted and rebel under the leadership of Gog and Magog. There is their annihilation and the time of Great White Throne Judgment. We are not privy to how long this takes. We do know that after this the influence of evil is finally disposed.

THE NEW HEAVEN AND EARTH.

There can be confusion about the placement of the New Heaven and Earth in prophecy. Some believe it follows the Tribulation's end. Others believe it is at the Millennium's end. Note these two accounts.

Isa 65:17-25   For, behold, **I create new heavens and a new earth**: *and the former shall not be remembered, nor come into mind.*:18 But be ye glad and rejoice for ever in that which I create: for, behold, **I create Jerusalem a rejoicing**, and her people a joy.:19 And I will rejoice in Jerusalem, and joy in my people: and the voice of weeping shall be no more heard in her, nor the voice of crying.:20 There shall be no more thence an infant of days, nor an old man that hath not filled his days: for the child shall die an hundred years old; but the sinner being an hundred years old shall be accursed.:21 And they shall build houses, and inhabit them; and they shall plant vineyards, and eat the fruit of them.:22 They shall not build, and another inhabit; they shall not plant, and another eat: for as the days of a tree are the days of my people, and mine elect shall long enjoy the work of their hands.:23 They shall not labour in vain, nor bring forth for trouble; for they are the seed of the blessed of the LORD, and their offspring with them.:24 And it shall come to pass, that before they call, I will answer; and while they are yet speaking, I will hear.:25

The wolf and the lamb shall feed together, and the lion shall eat straw like the bullock: and dust shall be the serpent's meat. They shall not hurt nor destroy in all my holy mountain, saith the LORD.

Rev 20:15 And whosoever was not found written in the book of life was cast into the lake of fire. **Rev 21:1** And **I saw a new heaven and a new earth**: for the first heaven and the first earth were passed away; and there was no more sea.:2 **And I John saw the holy city, new Jerusalem**, coming down from God out of heaven, prepared as a bride adorned for her husband.:3 And I heard a great voice out of heaven saying, Behold, the tabernacle of God is with men, and he will dwell with them, and they shall be his people, and God himself shall be with them, and be their God.:4 And God shall wipe away all tears from their eyes; and there shall be no more death, neither sorrow, nor crying, neither shall there be any more pain: *for the former things are passed away.*

At first glance there would seem to be some contradictions but with a closer look you will see they cover different issues. First, it is important to notice these scriptures not only speak of a New Heaven and Earth but also of Jerusalem. The prophecies concerning Jerusalem are not the same. Rev.21 speaks of a New Jerusalem coming down from heaven. The account in Isaiah speaks of a Jerusalem on earth. The subject of a New Heaven and Earth actually ends in the same verse in Isaiah 65v17 and the remaining eight verses speak about earthly Jerusalem and the joy God will make it. In this Jerusalem death still reigns. Not so in Rev.21. Isaiah 65 account is the Jerusalem of the millennium kingdom. The account in revelation is the crown of the New Heaven And Earth when the millennium ends.

PART 3.
MAJOR
CHARACTERS

You really can't judge a book by its cover.
You have to see its back yard. (Math 7:16)

QUESTIONS TO PONDER.

1. What kinds of vehicles does God use to
   work His will?
2. What does God reveal to us through
   symbols and types?

9
The White Horse Riders

We've learned and seen thus far truth is consistent in the word of God. Without consistency in symbols and revelation there is only confusion. Since God is not the author of confusion we must be careful not to create a double standard by adjusting symbols to fit our theory or interpretation. Our job is to investigate the facts and connect them as best we can. We may err in our rendition but let us not be guilty of tampering with the evidence. There are two White Horse riders mentioned in the book of Revelation.

And I saw heaven opened, and behold a white horse; and he that sat upon him *was* called Faithful and True, and in righteousness he doth judge and make war.

His eyes *were* as a flame of fire, and on his head *were* many crowns; and he had a name written, that no man knew, but he himself. And he *was* clothed with a vesture dipped in blood: and his name is called The Word of God. and the armies *which were* in heaven followed him upon white horses, clothed in fine linen, white and clean.

And out of his mouth goeth a sharp sword, that with it he should smite the nations: and he shall rule them with a rod of iron: and he treadeth the winepress of the fierceness and wrath of Almighty God. And he hath on *his* vesture and on his thigh a name written, KING OF KINGS, AND LORD OF LORDS. (Rev 19:11-16KJV)

This is none other than Jesus Christ in the book of Rev chapter 19. In verse 17-19 we see Him returning from judging the earth. He sits on a white horse; on His head are many crowns. The Armies of Heaven are clothed in fine white linen upon white horses.

Rev chapter 6 reveals another White Horse rider with a crown and a bow. The horses recorded in the scriptures were mainly used as vehicles for warfare. White is the color of purity and righteousness. We also must note that all four horses of Rev 6 are symbols of the Spirits of Heaven that go to and fro in the earth. (Zech. 1:8-11 & 6:2-5) For consistency of scripture the white horse is a vehicle for divine justice and deliverance. (Rev.19:11 & 14) There is not a symbol of wickedness or evil mentioned on a white horse or related with one in the word of God. Just the opposite is true. So who is the rider of Rev 6? This scripture gives us a clue to His identity.

(Isa 28:5-6 KJV) In that day shall the LORD of hosts be for a crown of glory, and for a diadem of beauty, unto the residue of his people,:6 And for a spirit of judgment to him that sitteth in judgment, and for strength to them that turn the battle to the gate.

Here we see our Lord with a single crown of glory in "That Day," in the spirit of judgment and strength to battle. The word of God tells us in Acts 2:34 & 3:21, that Jesus until the time of restoration sits on right hand of the father until his enemies are made His footstool. This does not mean Jesus is immobilized in a chair in heaven. Its symbolic, "sits on my right hand," meaning place of honor and acquittal. (Matt 25:33) This means heaven is now his place of residence & honor. That will change when all things are restored on earth. Acts 2:34 is quoting (Psa 110:1-2 KJV)

A Psalm of David. The LORD said unto my Lord, Sit thou at my right hand, until I make thine enemies thy footstool. The LORD shall send the rod of thy strength out of Zion: rule thou in the midst of thine enemies.

These words are important, "Rule in the midst of your enemies." We already see God can make conquest by whatever vehicle he desires. God is seen dealing through human and natural agencies to pour out judgment upon the earth. In Rev.ch 6:2 he goes out conquering and to conquer in the beginning of judgment. Listen to the prayer of Habakkuk the prophet upon Shigionoth.

Before him went the pestilence, and burning coals went forth at his feet. He stood, and measured the earth: he beheld, and drove asunder the nations; and the everlasting mountains were scattered, the perpetual hills did bow: his ways *are* everlasting. Was the LORD displeased against the rivers? *was* thine anger against the rivers? *was* thy wrath against the sea, that thou didst ride upon thine horses *and* thy chariots of salvation?

Thy bow was made quite naked, *according* to the oaths of the tribes, *even thy* word. Selah. Thou didst cleave the earth with rivers. The mountains saw thee, *and* they trembled: the overflowing of the water passed by: the deep uttered his voice, *and* lifted up his hands on high. The sun *and* moon stood still in their habitation: at the light of thine arrows they went, *and* at the shining of thy glittering spear.

Thou didst march through the land in indignation, thou didst thresh the heathen in anger. Thou wentest forth for the salvation of thy people, *even* for salvation with thine anointed; thou woundedst the head out of the house of the wicked, by discovering the foundation unto the neck. Selah. Thou didst strike through with his staves the head of his villages: they came out as a whirlwind to scatter me: their rejoicing *was* as to devour the poor secretly.

Thou didst walk through the sea with thine horses, *through* the heap of great waters. When I heard, my belly trembled; my lips quivered at the voice: rottenness entered into my bones, and I trembled in myself, **that I might rest in the day of trouble**: when he cometh up unto the people, he will invade them with his troops. (Hab 3v5-16 KJV)

Here we have two pictures of our Lord, before and after. Habakkuk's prophecy speaks of the "midst of years " and the day of trouble. Christ goes forth at the beginning of the tribulation in the spirit of judgment, He has come out before the final battle. He has with him the spoils of victory. Verses 12 & 13 say he doth judge and make war. In Rev 6 he is conquering to conquer. He goes forth with one crown but he returns with many. He departs to conquer -- He returns with blood up to his thigh.

(Isa 63:1-3 KJV) Who *is* this that cometh from Edom, with dyed garments from Bozrah? this *that is* glorious in his apparel, travelling in the greatness of his strength? I that speak in righteousness, mighty to save. *{2}* Wherefore *art thou* red in thine apparel, and thy garments like him that treadeth in the winefat? *{3}* I have trodden the winepress alone; and of the people *there was* none with me: for I will tread them in mine anger, and trample them in my fury; and their blood shall be sprinkled upon my garments, and I will stain all my raiment

Jude 14-15 It appears not all the saints are going to battle -- just a select few. Deut.33v2.

10
THE FOUR HORSEMEN

The bible tells us these four Horseman of Rev.6 are **Four Spirits of Heaven**. (Zech 6:1-7) The Horse in ancient Hebrew times as recorded in the Bible was mostly used for military purposes. (Isa 36:28, 2 kings 19:28, Psalm 32:9, Proverbs 26:3, Job 39:19 –25) The issue in these texts is heavens judgment. Here in Rev 6 God explains clearly their purpose.

Death & Hell on a pale green horse; **Famine** & inflation on a black horse; and **War** on a red horse. **Man with bow** on white has by many been referred to as the antichrist coming with peace but is deceiving in true intentions. This view has no scriptural support. (See White horse rider.)
The scripture reveals the Lord has been seen in battle both in chariots and on horseback. Hab3:8, Rev 19:11–12 and with bows and arrows. Hab 3:9&11, Psalms 18:14.Ezk.5v15-16.

The issue to examine is his purpose, conquering & to conquer. (Rev.6v2). The Greek word Nikao is defined; means by which victory comes -- to subdue, conquer and overcome. This word's usage throughout the New Testament always refers to the victory of Christ and his followers. It's also important to note they are the methods (means) God uses for judgment.
I mention this because the four horsemen are the only figurative characters mentioned in the judgments. All the woe judgments are literal in context. So are the trumpets & vials. John sees these symbols in the first four seals.

THE FOUR HOURSEMEN ARE
SYMBOLS OF COMING EVENTS

John sees actual events in the others and describes them with the knowledge of man living in his time period. (God knew we'd get the message). This is not symbolic of Christ leaving his place. (Acts3v21) These are the spirits of heaven bringing forth the prophetic word of God. What we see in the four horsemen of Rev.6 is the same **judgment for defiling the sanctuary** in Ezek. chpt. 5.

(Ezek 5:11-13 KJV) Wherefore, *as* I live, saith the Lord GOD; Surely, *because thou hast defiled my sanctuary with all thy detestable things, and with all thine abominations,* therefore will I also diminish *thee;* neither shall mine eye spare, neither will I have any pity. *{12}* A third part of thee shall die with the pestilence, and with famine shall they be consumed in the midst of thee: and a third part shall fall by the sword round about thee; and I will scatter a third part into all the winds, and I will draw out a sword after them (prophecy concerning Israel).

We also see similar judgments for covenant breaking and hindering of worship.Ex.5v3, Lev26v15-16&21-32, 1Chr21v6-12, Ezk5v11-17. God calls His judgments furious rebukes in Ezk.5v14. Jesus said in Math Chpt.24 the **defiling of the sanctuary would mark the Great Tribulation.**

There are great similarities in these two prophecies (Rev.ch6 & Ezk.ch5). Both tribulations are not from man but from heaven and the vehicles of these judgments are sometimes called arrows in prophecy. These arrows can come by natural calamity or human means. Observe the text in Ezk.5v16.

(Ezek 5:16-17 KJV) When I shall send upon them the evil arrows of famine, which shall be for *their* destruction, *and* which I will send to destroy you: and I will increase the famine upon you, and will break your staff of bread: {17} So will I send upon you famine and evil beasts, and they shall bereave thee; and pestilence and blood shall pass through thee; and I will bring the sword upon thee. I the LORD have spoken it.(Also Psm18v14)

I don't think its by chance the 1ˢᵗ judgments (trumpet & vial) are hail, fire and pestilence on the Beast's kingdom. Hab3v5 says before him (The Lord) went pestilence, and burning coals went forth at his feet. Habakkuk shows this happening before the day of trouble, the Lord invading with his army. Habakkuk also tells us the rider's bow will be made naked or empty (hab.3v9). The word Qesheth in Hebrew means bending bow while eryah and uwr means made empty. The picture is the Lord riding through tribulation firing His arrows.

The woe judgments (final 3 judgments) are by the divine hand of God. They're the Locust; Day of the Lord- for which Armageddon is the setting, plus fire. (Rev 8v13) Yet these first four judgments are different. These are events that have come by the decisions of man. "It is the sin of man that has brought forth these creations". It was man's disobedience that brought to pass God's judgment. In the last days we see the apex of man's sin and God's judgment upon it.

(Heb 2:2 KJV) For if the word spoken by angels was steadfast, and every transgression and disobedience received a just recompense of reward;(:3) How shall we escape, if we neglect so great salvation; which at the first began to be spoken by the Lord, and was confirmed unto us by them that heard *him;*

THEIR IDENTITIES
We have the White horse. The Conqueror ....
Rev6v2 Symbolic of God initiating wrath on the children of disobedience and the pride of man. (Eph 5:5-6 & Col 3:56 & Ex 15:26)

(Deu 32:42 KJV) I will make mine arrows drunk with blood, and my sword shall devour flesh; *and that* with the blood of the slain and of the captives, from the beginning of revenges upon the enemy.

The first trumpet shows coals of fire with blood, and one third of all vegetation on earth is destroyed -- instant famine.
The first vial shows pestilence on the kingdom of the beast, the initial rebuke for the antichrist's actions and his displeasure with Israel's covenant with him. Zeph3v7-8 .

The Red Horse War ....No peace....Rev6v4
(James 4:1 KJV) From whence *come* wars and fightings among you? *come they* not hence, *even* of your lusts that war in your members? (2) Ye lust, and have not: ye kill, and desire to have, and cannot obtain: ye fight and war, yet ye have not, because ye ask not.(:3) Ye ask, and receive not, because ye ask amiss, that ye may consume *it* upon your lusts. Also Ex. 15:9-10 & Rom 7:21-23,

Ezk.5 tells us one third shall fall by sword, which is symbolic of war. The Horsemen in revelation is given a great sword to take away peace. Be it for greatness, power, greed or spoil its all a sample of mans evil heart. For this reason the righteous must rage war. For only when evil is overcome shall war stop. The term "a third part" is a measurement often used in the bible for sacrifice and service. Num15v6-7, 2Chron23v45, Nehm10v32

(Psa 46:8 KJV) Come, behold the works of the LORD, what desolations he hath made in the earth.(:9) He maketh wars to cease unto the end of the earth; he breaketh the bow, and cutteth the spear in sunder; he burneth the chariot in the fire.(:10) Be still, and know that I *am* God: I will be exalted among the heathen, I will be exalted in the earth.

61

Black horse of morning & woe...Famine.....Rev6v5
One denarius for a bag of groceries, a penny (Matthew 20:2) a
day's wages in those days. This is inflation -- the increase of
cost. We see this is also very similar to Ezekiel's
prophecy...*and I will increase the famine upon you, and will
break your staff of bread:* .. (Ezek 5:16 KJV) Here we see and
additional famine added with inflation 'break your staff of
bread"(See Ezk.4v16) God calls all men to know the pangs of
lack at this point of the Tribulation.   Micah. 6:11-14. James 5:1-6

Finally Death with Hell following,..Rev6v8
Because of one man's sin, this pale greenish judgment is
followed by Hades. This is where the wicked depart before the
lake of fire. Physical death followed by eternal death (Eternal
separation from God) to await eternal torment.

(Rev 6:8 KJV) And I looked, and behold a pale horse: and his name that
sat on him was Death, and Hell followed with him. And power was given
unto them over the fourth part of the earth, to kill with sword, and with
hunger, and with death, and with the beasts of the earth.

We see this also in Ezk. (Ezek 5:17 KJV) So will I send upon you
famine and evil beasts, and they shall bereave thee; and pestilence and
blood (bloodshed) shall pass through thee; and I will bring the sword upon
thee. I the LORD have spoken *it*.

Death and hell are connected in they're workings and destinies.
Rev20v13-14 Jesus gives us insight to Hades Lk16v22-31; it's a
place of flame and torment, yet this is not the lake of fire.

11
THE THRONE ROOM

THE ELDERS

In Rev ch4 we see the throne room. A throne surrounded by twenty four others. He who sat on the throne v8-9 is identified as the Lord God Almighty. "The Elders" sit on the twenty-four thrones. Who are they? Our hint lies in Rev. chapter 18. The angel reveals the destruction of Babylon and declares (Rev 18:20) the response in heaven at the announcement of her fall. The Holy Apostles and Prophets. Rev19:4-5 records the same event calling them the Elders.

(Mat 19:27 KJV) Then answered Peter and said unto him, Behold, we have forsaken all, and followed thee; what shall we have therefore? (:28) And Jesus said unto them, Verily I say unto you, That ye which have followed me, in the regeneration when the Son of man shall sit in the throne of his glory, ye also shall sit upon twelve thrones, judging the twelve tribes of Israel.

(Rev 4:3 KJV) And he that sat was to look upon like a jasper and a sardine stone: and *there was* a rainbow round about the throne, in sight like unto an emerald. (4) And round about the throne *were* four and twenty seats: and upon the seats I saw four and twenty elders sitting, clothed in white raiment; and they had on their heads crowns of gold.

(1 Chr 24:19 KJV) These *were* the orderings of them in their service to come into the house of the LORD, according to their manner, under Aaron their father, as the LORD God of Israel had commanded him. 24 is the number representing the entire priesthood...also 1Chr24v1-4

(Luke 22:29 KJV) And I appoint unto you a kingdom, as my Father hath appointed unto me;(30) That ye may eat and drink at my table in my kingdom, and sit on thrones judging the twelve tribes of Israel.

(Exo 19:6 KJV) And ye shall be unto me a kingdom of priests, and an holy nation. These *are* the words which thou shalt speak unto the children of Israel.

THE FOUR BEASTS

The Four Beasts. (Ezek.1:5-11, Rev.4:6-11.)These are powerful Angels and they are holy. In them we see the fourfold revelation of our Lord -- symbols of His divine character and personality. We find our Lord portrayed as these individual faces in the scriptures. A careful study of each gospel will also show a dominating parallel characteristic with each creature.

The Lion of Judah presented in gospel of Matthew. The Royalty of our Lord. (Rev5v5) **The Ox**, The Servant, book of Mark. (Math 11v29) **The Man**, The Humanity of Christ presented by the physician Luke. (Isa7v14) **The Eagle**, Divinity of Jesus Christ presented in the gospel of John. (Deut32v11)

These creations are closest to the throne of God. Yet the vision of Ezekiel differs in that they had four faces each. John accounts one face per creature.

The uniqueness of John's vision is that each beast brings forth one of the first four Seal judgments which are the Horsemen of the Apocalypse. Notice in chapter four John assigns numbers to them. In Chpt.6 v1-3-5& 7 you see that particular beast revealing a particular judgment.

HE WHO SITS ON THE THRONE.

Rev 4:3 And he that sat was to look upon like a jasper and a sardine stone: and there was a rainbow round about the throne, in sight like unto an emerald.

Jasper is one of the twelve precious stones used to represent the children of Israel. *(The tribe of Asher, Exo 28:20)* It makes up part of the foundation of the New Jerusalem and also symbolizes the twelve tribes as well as the entire wall. Jasper is known for its clarity, "as clear as crystal." (Rev 21:18-19). In the likeness of sardine and Jasper we see God on the throne. The rainbow symbolizes His commitment to His covenants.

THE SEA OF GLASS
Rev 4:6 And before the throne there was a sea of glass like unto crystal: and in the midst of the throne,

This is a special place reserved by God for His Martyrs -- those murdered for their testimony in the Great Tribulation. They shall sing a new song .... Great and marvellous are thy works, Lord God Almighty; just and true are thy ways, thou King of saints. Who shall not fear thee, O Lord, and glorify thy name? for thou only art holy: for all nations shall come and worship before thee; for thy judgments are made manifest. (Rev 15:2-4)

This event serves as a marker for the beginning and ending of the Tribulation. It also reveals God's tremendous love, patience and mercy to those who are slow to respond.

12
ANGEL WITH A RAINBOW

The Angel with a rainbow about his Head (Rev.10)

Here we see Jesus Himself appearing with a rainbow about his head, which represents a covenant. (Gen.9v12-13) Coming with a cloud is symbolic of the second coming of Christ with the saints. *Dan7v13, Jude v14-15, Rev14v14.*Gods glory. *Ex.40v35, 1Kings 8v10-11* His feet are pillars of fire, with His right foot on the sea left upon earth, a posture of standing in judgment over his creation. Hag 2v6, Acts 4v24

(Psa 75:2 KJV) When I shall receive the congregation I will judge uprightly. (:3) The earth and all the inhabitants thereof are dissolved: I bear up the pillars of it. Selah.

The Seven Thunders are the voices of God's judgments Ex.9v34, Job.40v9, Psa. 77v18, 1Sam.12v17. Seven means complete. The words uttered John was not permitted to write, but he tells us that in the days the Seventh Angel begins to sound, the mystery of God shall be finished. Notice how he brings in…. "Seventh angel sounded."

"(Rev 11:15 KJV) And the seventh angel sounded; and there were great voices in heaven, saying, The kingdoms of this world are become *the kingdoms* of our Lord, and of his Christ; and he shall reign for ever and ever. (Rev 11:18 KJV) And the nations were angry, and thy wrath is come, and the time of the dead, that they should be judged, and that thou shouldest give reward unto thy servants the prophets, and to the saints, and them that fear thy name, small and great; and shouldest destroy them which destroy the earth.

It is finished -- the words of our Lord before resurrection.

Finally we come to the little book. God gives us a parallel in Ezk 1v28

(Ezek 1:28 KJV) As the appearance of the bow that is in the cloud in the day of rain, so *was* the appearance of the brightness round about. This *was* the appearance of the likeness of the glory of the LORD. And when I saw *it,* I fell upon my face, and I heard a voice of one that spake.

We see the same symbolism in Ezk 3v1-3. Like John, Ezekiel is required to eat the book. The book in Ezekiel is not a mystery. (Ezek 2:9 KJV) Most men take pleasure in seeing the future unfold, "A word in due season how good it is!" But once digested and when the reality of what is to come is fully realized, it can be a somber and bitter pill to swallow.

13
THE TALE OF TWO BEASTS

DANIEL'S FOURTH BEAST IS NOT JOHN'S (Review Dan.2:31-35 & 7:1-8)

(Rev 13:1-2 KJV) And I stood upon the sand of the sea, and saw a beast rise up out of the sea, having seven heads and ten horns, and upon his horns ten crowns, and upon his heads the name of blasphemy. {2} And the beast which I saw was like unto a leopard, and his feet were as the feet of a bear, and his mouth as the mouth of a lion: and the dragon gave him his power, and his seat, and great authority.

In Rev.13 we find the Beast with seven heads. The question is who is the beast? We are given clues.

(Rev 17:8 KJV) The beast that thou sawest was, and is not; and shall ascend out of the bottomless pit, and go into perdition: and they that dwell on the earth shall wonder, whose names were not written in the book of life from the foundation of the world, when they behold the beast that was, and is not, and yet is......(Rev 17:11-13 KJV) And the beast that was, and is not, even he is the eighth, and is of the seven, and goeth into perdition. {12} And the ten horns which thou sawest are ten kings, which have received no kingdom as yet; but receive power as kings one hour with the beast. {13} These have one mind, and shall give their power and strength unto the beast.

The mystery words "beast that was and is not yet is": Many have taken this to be the beast of Daniel ch7 v 7-8 & v 23. THIS IS AN INCORRECT interpretation. This misinterpretation has Christians looking for a ten-nation confederation and many other false signs. Its important to remember that before God describes the fourth kingdom as a Beast.(Dan.ch7v23) He gives a parallel vision in Dan.ch.2v40-44.

(Dan 2:40-44 KJV) And the fourth kingdom shall be strong as iron: forasmuch as iron breaketh in pieces and subdueth all *things:* and as iron that breaketh all these, shall it break in pieces and bruise. *{41}* And whereas thou sawest the feet and toes, part of potters' clay, and part of iron, the kingdom shall be divided; but there shall be in it of the strength of the iron, forasmuch as thou sawest the iron mixed with miry clay. *{42}* And *as* the toes of the feet *were* part of iron, and part of clay, *so* the kingdom shall be partly strong, and partly broken. *{43}* And whereas thou sawest iron mixed with miry clay, they shall mingle themselves with the seed of men: but they shall not cleave one to another, even as iron is not mixed with clay. *{44}* And in the days of these kings shall the God of heaven set up a kingdom, which shall never be destroyed: and the kingdom shall not be left to other people, *but* it shall break in pieces and consume all these kingdoms, and it shall stand for ever.

The Kingdom of Iron history has shown to be the Roman Empire. Rome is the next great empire following the Greeks. (The male goat of Dan8v8 & v21) Yet there is a division of Kings & Kingdoms. (Dan. 2v41 & 44) Notice " In day of these Kings."

Dan 7:24 KJV) And the ten horns out of this kingdom *are* ten kings *that* shall arise: and another shall rise after them; and he shall be diverse from the first, and he shall subdue three kings.

Notice also "another after them," a time to come. From here Dan 7 goes on to identify him as the antichrist. The beast as we established earlier means ruling King and Kingdom (Empire). The empire of the Iron legs that devoured the nations has passed. The beast of John is the beast of iron and clay. The Kingdom of the Eleventh Horn. The Beast that according to Revelation is like the first but is not, yet is. Note the difference between Daniel's and John's. (Daniel's has one head – John's has 7 heads) (Daniel's 10 horns are Kings of the Kingdom- John's 10 horns are people outside his Kingdom) (Daniel's

Beast is different from other Kingdoms-John's beast is a combination of the previous Kingdoms.)

(Rev 13:2 KJV) And the beast which I saw was like unto a leopard, and his feet were as *the feet* of a bear, and his mouth as the mouth of a lion: and the dragon gave him his power, and his seat, and great authority......the iron mixed with clay .

These Beasts in the bible also symbolize time frames. Each represented a point in history. Here lies the danger of interpreting a wrong time period. Daniel 2v44 tells us in the days of the iron and clay Kings, the everlasting kingdom is set up (which designates a time period). In Daniel God reveals the last kingdom of Nebuchadnezzar's dream is broken into two time periods. The legs of Iron represent old Roman empire-the 4th beast of Daniel. The feet of Iron and clay represent John's beast -- the revised Roman empire of the end times. Another common misinterpretation is the emphasis placed on the ten toes of Iron and clay. We don't focus on the two knees or legs as separate nations within old Roman Empire. (Though some might attempt to) Why place significance on the toes as various member nations or kingdoms? In the book of Revelation John makes no comment on the size or membership within the Beast's Kingdom. John does give a list of his allies.

The Bible makes clear John's Beast is also a man, one of the seven leaders of this empire. (Rev 17:11-13 KJV) He goes by many names in the word of God. *Anti Christ,(1 John 2:18 KJV) Man of Sin , Son of perdition. 2 these 2v3 ,vile person, Dan. 11v2-40, Prince that shall come. Dan 9v 26.lawless one.2thess.2v8 ,little horn of Dan7v8 and the Assyrian.*

II John 1v7 tells us the spirit of antichrist is to deny that Christ has come. He will claim this appointment for himself -- the anointed one of God.

(2 Th 2:3-4 KJV) Let no man deceive you by any means: for *that day shall not come,* except there come a falling away first, and that man of sin be revealed, the son of perdition; *{4}* Who opposeth and exalteth himself above all that is called God, or that is worshipped; so that he as God sitteth in the temple of God, showing himself that he is God.

This beast also fulfills the Abomination of Desolation recorded in Math 24 and Dan 7v25. Note also the 3 ½ yrs. reference in Daniel.

The picture we have is the beast of the last days, a descendent of the old Roman Empire. The beast represents the iron and clay time period. Iron and clay is symbolic of peoples. Job 13v12, Isa.26v16 and 2nd Corth.4v7 .He will come from and lead this empire. He will be empowered by the dragon (devil). The book of Daniel gives us some insight to his personality and character.

(Dan 11:36-38 KJV) And the king shall do according to his will; and he shall exalt himself, and magnify himself above every god, and shall speak marvellous things against the God of gods, and shall prosper till the indignation be accomplished: for that that is determined shall be done. *{37}* Neither shall he regard the God of his fathers, nor the desire of women, nor regard any god: for he shall magnify himself above all. *{38}* But in his estate shall he honour the God of forces: and a god whom his fathers knew not shall he honour with gold, and silver, and with precious stones, and pleasant things

I also believe it is important to note that he will break the "Holy Covenant". (Dan.11v30) This league or covenant seems to be partly religious in nature. It also includes military strength.

(Dan 11:23-24 KJV) And after the league *made* with him he shall work deceitfully: for he shall come up, and shall become strong with a small people. *{24}* He shall enter peaceably even upon the fattest places of the province; and he shall do *that* which his fathers have not done, nor his fathers' fathers; he shall scatter among them the prey, and spoil, and riches: *yea,* and he shall forecast his devices against the strong holds, even for a time.

The beast also comes to power, not as a person of honor but through diplomacy and eventually disbands his opposition by military might. (Dan11v21-22)
Dan7v8 seems to give a geographical location.
Its also important to remember the beast (kingdom) is not a kingdom until it is united and under one leader. The bible is clear this kingdom will have seven leaders and one will have two terms, the antichrist. This is consistent with the book of Daniel's "vile one" and "the beast" of Rev. Compare text.

(Rev 17:10-11 KJV) And there are seven kings: five are fallen, and one is, *and* the other is not yet come; and when he cometh, he must continue a short space. *{11}* And the beast that was, and is not, even he is the eighth, and is of the seven, and goeth into perdition

(Dan 11:19-21 KJV) Then he shall turn his face toward the fort of his own land: but he shall stumble and fall, and not be found. *{20}* Then shall stand up in his estate a raiser of taxes *in* the glory of the kingdom: but within few days he shall be destroyed, neither in anger, nor in battle. *{21}* And in his estate shall stand up a vile person, to whom they shall not give the honour of the kingdom: but he shall come in peaceably, and obtain the kingdom by flatteries. There is a break in time from ancient civilization to modern. Dan11v7, like Rev17, begins with the sixth king or leader.

TEN HORNS   **Rev17v12-13&16-17**
The beast has a relationship with ten leaders with no nations. The Beast is also known for the religious system it supports. The bible calls it the Harlot, (see pg.71) which is the focus of the Ten Horns. The opening is very important in the placement of the end time events. We start with "Babylon The Great Whore has fallen." The Harlot has been destroyed by the Ten Horns.

(Rev 17v16) The Ten Horns will receive power as kings with their alliance to the Beast. What's important to note here is the Ten are in unity, "they hate her." They're geographically not a part of the beast kingdom, yet they execute military power. The destruction of the harlot happens in Armageddon, which suggests this is their one-hour of power with the beast.

(Rev 18:18 KJV) And cried when they saw the smoke of her burning, saying, What *city is* like unto this great city!

(Rev 18:20-21 KJV) Rejoice over her, *thou* heaven, and *ye* holy apostles and prophets; for God hath avenged you on her. *{21}* And a mighty angel took up a stone like a great millstone, and cast *it* into the sea, saying, Thus with violence shall that great city Babylon be thrown down, and shall be found no more at all.

Prophecies in the Old Testament sometimes refer to Conquerors of Babylon as the Spoilers (Jerm.51:56-58, Isa 21:2-3&9) meaning one who lays waste. God uses these kings to bring His judgment. What's also important is this order is consistent in scripture.

Rev. Chapter 19 Babylon Fall, Wedding Feast, Wine press of wrath..
(Destruction of the unrepentant)
Rev. Chapter 14 Babylon Fall, Warning don't take the mark, Wine press..

Interesting note: Jerm 51:63. We see later how prophetic this is. Joel chapter 2 reveals (concerning these events) a great battle, the wedding feast and then a call to judge the heathen. This reveals that tribulation martyrs will not attend the wedding feast. This celebration is clearly for the church (bride). I believe what we see in Revelation chpt.19 is a heavenly view of The Day of The Lord. I say this because Armageddon is the setting of The Day of the Lord. It is during the battle of Armageddon that Mystery Babylon falls.

Rev 16 v19 records a final Judgment for Babylon after 7th judgment sounded. The 6th judgment shows all mankind seeking refuge.
The warfare of men has ended thus the judgment of ch18:9 would be separate from that of ch16. *(Rev18:21 could be the 2nd judgment recorded in ch16)*

THE SECOND BEAST

(Rev 13:11-12 KJV) And I beheld another beast coming up out of the earth; and he had two horns like a lamb, and he spake as a dragon. {12} And he exerciseth all the power of the first beast before him, and causeth the earth and them which dwell therein to worship the first beast, whose deadly wound was healed.

This is a dominating ruling kingdom in the same time period as the first beast. It comes from the earth. The first beast comes from the sea, (bottomless pit) which relates to Daniel's original beast. (Dan. 7v3) This beast is **a combination of two kings and kingdoms** (two horns). They look like a lamb. This is symbolic of Jesus Christ. *John1v29. Acts.8v32, 1Pet.19v20.* Yet we are told it speaks like a dragon -- the devil. (Rev12v9). They have great power to do signs and set up an image of the first beast. They are also responsible for instituting the mark, number and name of the first beast. (Rev 13:13-17 KJV)

We have two nations that are world powers during the time of the beast. They look CHRIST LIKE but speak like devils. (Mth.15v18).
They promote the first beast and give power to his image that it might be worshiped. They are united and have the technology to institute a worldwide identification system. They have power over the world economies. The bible calls them THE FALSE PROPHET.Rev.19v20,,13v14

14
THE WORLD'S WITNESS

The Two Witnesses (Rev 11)

Zec 4:11 Then answered I, and said unto him, What are these two olive trees upon the right side of the candlestick and upon the left side thereof? :12 And I answered again, and said unto him, What be these two olive branches which through the two golden pipes empty the golden oil out of themselves?:13 And he answered me and said, Knowest thou not what these be? And I said, No, my lord.:14 Then said he, These are the two anointed ones, that stand by the Lord of the whole earth.

There are two destinies finely entwined into one throughout the book of Revelation -- the church & Israel. The first three chapters of the book of Revelation concerns the church. Jesus calls them seven candlesticks. This is symbolic of their witness, a light in the darkness. (Rev 1v20 & 2v1)
Just as the world received a witness from the church they shall also receive one from Israel. (Rev 11v4) Who are they? We can identify one from the scripture. Many commentators place Moses or Enoch as the other.

Mal 4:5 Behold, I will send you Elijah the prophet before the coming of the great and dreadful day of the LORD::6 And he shall turn the heart of the fathers to the children, and the heart of the children to their fathers, lest I come and smite the earth with a curse.

They shall be more than witnesses. They give the oil by which fires are lit. **They are the candlestick** -- God's light to the world. As Jesus dwelled in the midst of the candlesticks of the church, these two will provide the oil for what our Lord does in the tribulation. They're called Olive Trees -- a symbol of Hebrew heritage. These men will be prophets and will have worldwide authority.

The Jewish destiny begins with a "covenant hand shake". During this seven-year countdown two witnesses appear in Israel with a 31\2 year ministry. Malachi says they come before dreadful day of the Lord, The Second Coming. This aligned with the 6th Trumpet *(Rev.11v14)* tells us their ministry ends the same hour the second "Woe" is past. This next judgment is the battle of Armageddon as we will study later. This tells us their ministry begins sometime before abomination that makes desolate. *(Dan 12 gives a time span).* Their ministry according to Malachi is to turn the father to the children and children to father. It is also to bring the Jewish people back into right relationship with the heavenly father and bear witness of Jesus the Christ.

Another clue is found in Mth17:10-11. "Note" This is after the beheading of John. Some have envisioned these men materializing from heaven as at the Mount of Transfiguration. We have no evidence of how they will arrive or if they will come in the spirit of Elijah like John or be Old Testament prophets *(who arrive as in the transfiguration)* We do know their 3 1\2 year ministry will stop rainfall, turn water to blood, bring plagues and fire will fall on their enemies just like Elijah & Moses. The text is literal! (Rev 2-5) Notice also there is a connection with Holy city being trampled which also confirms the time in which they minister.

John, at the opening of Rev.11, is told to measure the temple yet not the court. He is also told to measure the people that worship there. What John was not told to measure would be under the dominance of Gentile powers. This possibly implies the temple will survive this season and those that worship at its Altar. (Rev.11v1-2) The Altar is symbolic of Christ. This also shows the witnesses in sackcloth a sign of mourning in Jerusalem.

The 144,000

(Rev 14:4-5 KJV) These are they which were not defiled with women; for they are virgins. These are they which follow the Lamb whithersoever he goeth. These were redeemed from among men, being the firstfruits unto God and to the Lamb :5 And in their mouth was found no guile: for they are without fault before the throne of God.

They bring hope to the end time generation. They declare the true Messiah! They are the world's evangelists during the tribulation period. Their identity is made clear in Rev 7 -- twelve thousand men from each of the twelve tribes of Israel. Rev 7v 9 shows us the conclusion of their ministry before the Seventh Seal, the final Judgment. The conclusion is wonderful. A great multitude in which no man could number is redeemed out of the Great Tribulation.

We are told the 144,000 are sealed with the seal of God. The word sealed means marked, kept secured, preserved. It's also a symbol of authority. History tells us during the time period of the early church all Roman citizens were required to wear a signet ring. These were rings with impressions that identified you. *(Ref. Encarta Encyclo.)* Gold meant Roman by birth, silver meant freeman and iron meant free slave.

Example
(James 2:2 KJV) For if there come unto your assembly a man with a gold ring, in goodly apparel, and there come in also a poor man in vile raiment;

(Luke 15:22 KJV) But the father said to his servants, Bring forth the best robe, and put *it* on him; and put a ring on his hand, and shoes on *his* feet:

John the Baptist tells us this in John 3v33-34. He that hath received his testimony hath set to his seal that God is true. In ch.7v9 we see the seal of the 144,000.

(Rev 7:9 KJV) After this I beheld, and, lo, a great multitude, which no man could number, of all nations, and kindreds, and people, and tongues, stood before the throne, and before the Lamb, clothed with white robes, and palms in their hands;

Paul said this to the Corinthians (1 Cor 9:2 KJV) If I be not an apostle unto others, yet doubtless I am to you: for the seal of mine apostleship are ye in the Lord.

Here in chapter 14, we see 144,000 with the stamp of God on their forehead. (Rev7v3) The picture is they are standing with the lamb. The lamb is symbolic of Jesus our sacrificial lamb, Christ our redeemer. They are standing on Mt. Zion -- the place of the Temple. Jerusalem is called the city of God. Throughout scriptures Mt. Zion is a place of refuge and a place of deliverance. When we come under the blood of the Lamb we find refuge and deliverance. Hear the prophecies of Mt. Zion.

(Micah 4:7 KJV) And I will make her that halted a remnant, and her that was cast far off a strong nation: and the LORD shall reign over them in mount Zion from henceforth, even for ever.

(Joel 2:32 KJV) And it shall come to pass, *that* whosoever shall call on the name of the LORD shall be delivered: for in mount Zion and in Jerusalem shall be deliverance, as the LORD hath said, and in the remnant whom the LORD shall call.

On their forehead is the Father's name. Early on God required the Hebrew Priest to take a Gold plate and words were to be engraved on it like a signet ring of pure gold. It was to be worn on the forehead of his turban (Ex.28v 36-38). The purpose was a constant reminder of their priestly responsibility. The engraving on the plate said " Holiness To The Lord". Verse 4-5 talks of consecration. Men who in the darkest of times remain pure. Jewish converts, first fruits of the Jewish nation. *(Possibly converted by two witness)* They follow the Lamb wherever He goes. These are truly Christ missionaries to the nations. In a time of total insanity, war, disaster, their obedience doesn't waiver. These are not supermen, but humans who have answered the call of God for their lives. They are believers. They have a new song. The phrase new song is found nine times in the word of God. It revolves around the issue of salvation, God's deliverance and help.

(Rev 14:6 KJV) And I saw another angel fly in the midst of heaven, having the everlasting gospel to preach unto them that dwell on the earth, and to every nation, and kindred, and tongue, and people,

What they have experienced only God knows. God placed this section between the issues concerning the mark of the beast (Rev.13) and the three angels warning concerning the mark. (Rev.14v8-10) Here we see God's tremendous mercy. He has left the world in tribulation a witness. We don't know when their ministry begins. Rev 12 v6 suggests a preparation period and Rev 12v13-14, after the rapture of church, suggests dispersion. Praise be to God, for blessed are the feet of them that bring good news!

It is here we see Christianity at its basic requirement -- identifying with God. Those left on the earth are now faced clearly with the decision of Allegiance. The term being saved, born again, receiving salvation or whatever phrase one might use to describe a true child of God will be unnecessary. Your

79

church affiliation won't matter. The scriptures sum it up in a simple statement. You'll either identify with this world (mark) or suffer the reproach of the cross of Christ. You can lose your life and find it, or gain the world and lose your soul. How sad it is that even before the beast is manifest there are so called believers already bearing the mark of the world.

(Isa 66:19-22 KJV) And I will set a sign among them, and I will send those that escape of them unto the nations, *to* Tarshish, Pul, and Lud, that draw the bow, *to* Tubal, and Javan, *to* the isles afar off, that have not heard my fame, neither have seen my glory; and they shall declare my glory among the Gentiles. *{20}* And they shall bring all your brethren *for* an offering unto the LORD out of all nations upon horses, and in chariots, and in litters, and upon mules, and upon swift beasts, to my holy mountain Jerusalem, saith the LORD, as the children of Israel bring an offering in a clean vessel into the house of the LORD. *{21}* And I will also take of them for priests *and* for Levites, saith the LORD. *{22}* For as the new heavens and the new earth, which I will make, shall remain before me, saith the LORD, so shall your seed and your name remain.

15
The Woman of Rev. ch.12

We come now to a portion of scripture, which is truly a mystery. Some have claimed this woman, who is the central figure, represents the church of Jesus Christ, some the ecumenical movement. Others say she represents Eve and the seed that bruises the serpent's head. Still others say Israel. What's interesting is there are elements easily identified by those knowledgeable in the word of God.(v1-6)

The Dragon is Satan verse 3&9. The male child in verse 5 is Jesus Christ. Trying to place the events is the Great Mystery. One man has said these events are not in chronological order. I beg to differ. We serve a God of order.
Before identifying the woman let's identify the events.
I believe the event of Rev.12 is one concerning the Jewish people. I believe we are seeing a **Parallel of the Seventy weeks of Daniel's Vision.**

(Dan 9:24 KJV) Seventy weeks are determined upon thy people and upon thy holy city, to finish the transgression, and to make an end of sins, and to make reconciliation for iniquity, and to bring in everlasting righteousness, and to seal up the vision and prophecy, and to anoint the most Holy.

Look at the main points of this **prophecy: Dan ch.9**
Point 1. Restoration of the city to coming of Messiah = (reconciliation for
Iniquity)
    2. Messiah cut off   (v26)
    3. Final 7 yrs. divided by 3 1\2
    4. Covenant with Antichrist

5. Abomination Desolation: stops there with a mention this continues until judgment. (v27)

Note: The easily identifiable **parts of Rev12.**
Point 1. Messiah birth (v 5)
    2. Death & Resurrection (v 5) Break.

    3: (verse 6)
        3 1\2 prep. (7yrs. Divided by 3 1\2)
        31\2 escape. From. Presence of dragon (Anti-Christ)

Now let's look at the woman and walk through the events in scripture. Her identity and prophecy concerning her starts with the restoration of temple and extends to last day events.

The woman we find in (Isa 62:11 KJV)
Behold, the LORD hath proclaimed unto the end of the world, Say ye to the daughter of Zion, Behold, thy salvation cometh; behold, his reward is with him, and his work before him.(:12) And they shall call them, The holy people, The redeemed of the LORD: and thou shalt be called, Sought out, A city not forsaken.

Her name is **The Daughter of Zion.**
God told Daniel seventy weeks are determined for your people and the holy city. The Daughter of Zion is symbolic in scripture for the holy city and redeemed of the Lord. Isa 1v8-9, Lam 4v22, Lam 2v8.

It's important to note this prophecy in Isa.62 about a daughter of Zion is a prophecy about the restoration and the coming of Messiah. Isa 62:4, Dan.9:25 & Isa. 62:11*(This name has been given in scripture to describe Israel in this time period.)*

The woman wears a crown with 12 stars. The crown is symbolic of glory. (Prov 4:9 KJV) (Job 19:9 KJV) Job says stripped glory is like a crown removed, yet this woman in ch12 wears glory with twelve stars. Stars symbolize angelic hosts. Job 38:7, Jude 13. Israel and her leaders are called hosts and stars Dan 8v10-11. Twelve stars in Gen.37:9 symbolize the twelve tribes of Israel. The stars are a sign of heavenly glory upon the woman's head.

(Isa 62:1-3 KJV) For Zion's sake will I not hold my peace, and for Jerusalem's sake I will not rest, until the righteousness thereof go forth as brightness, and the salvation thereof as a lamp *that* burneth. {2} And the Gentiles shall see thy righteousness, and all kings thy glory: and thou shalt be called by a new name, which the mouth of the LORD shall name. {3} Thou shalt also be a crown of glory in the hand of the LORD, and a royal diadem in the hand of thy God. (4) Thou shalt no more be termed Forsaken; neither shall thy land any more be termed Desolate: but thou shalt be called Hephzibah, and thy land Beulah: for the LORD delighteth in thee, and thy land shall be married.

The sun symbolizes God's blessing and the moon a testimony of enduring, in which she is standing. Psm 89:37. Note some commentators have called the moon a symbol of idolatry. This is the mistake of discerning literal statement from figurative. God reveals to us the Daughter of Zion, a city and a people. We see their saga through the seventy weeks of Daniel.

THE DRAGONS FIRST FALL

Next we come to Rev 12:3-4 the devil, Satan. God reveals to us in John's vision the reason the dragon plots the child's destruction. It becomes clear in Ezekiel's Vision (Eziek 28:13-19). He was in the Garden of Eden. But he sinned against God, his sin being pride. God cast him to the ground. Verse 18 explains why a third of the stars in heaven fell also. In the garden he was judged and a promise given, Her seed will "bruise your head." Gen 3:15. Promises spoken to pride and as with all pride we see the insanity of his action. **He tries to devour the seed,** fighting against reveled truth.

Now we see the woman ready to give birth.

(Jer 4:31 KJV) For I have heard a voice as of a woman in travail, *and* the anguish as of her that bringeth forth her first child, the voice of the daughter of Zion, *that* bewaileth herself, *that* spreadeth her hands, *saying,* Woe *is* me now! for my soul is wearied because of murderers.

Micah 5:2-3. Dan 9:25 The prophecy ends with Destruction of the Temple. Then he goes in to final (week or 7 yrs).

Jer 6:4 Prepare ye war against her; arise, and let us go up at noon. Woe unto us! for the day goeth away, for the shadows of the evening are stretched out.:5 Arise, and let us go by night, and let us destroy her palaces.:6 For thus hath the LORD of hosts said, Hew ye down trees, and cast a mount against Jerusalem: this *is* the city to be visited; she *is* wholly oppression in the midst of her.:7 As a fountain casteth out her waters, so she casteth out her wickedness: violence and spoil is heard in her; before me continually *is* grief and wounds.:8 Be thou instructed, O Jerusalem, lest my soul depart from thee; lest I make thee desolate, a land not inhabited.

JERM6:1-3 gives another prophecy concerning the Daughter of Zion. First there's a warning of destruction from North, flee from Jerusalem. Then warnings for Tekoa and Beth Haccerem locations surrounding Bethlehem. Note (verse 1). This is possibly Herod's attempt to destroy Messiah. (Math 2:13-16). Yet at ch.6: 4 war breaks out and a picture perfect description come forth of Titus siege of Jerusalem 70 A D. In which city and sanctuary destroy.

We now come to the break in time. In both Dan & Rev 12 the story picks up with mention of 7yr period. Dan starts with the agreement but the content of the first 3 1\2 years is not mentioned. The focal point is the abomination that makes the desolate period. In Rev.12 the woman is in the wilderness 3 1\2 years in a special place prepared by God. The reason or event is not mentioned, possibly Ezk 20:33-37, but its focal point is the same as Daniel. In verse 7 another scene from heaven appears with the Dragon. Just as the previous scene was essential to understand the wrath against the child, this is also a forerunner to why the Beast breaks the covenant and is enraged with the woman and offspring. We know he is the beast because he is identified in Chpt.12:3, 13:1-2 & 17:9-14. He is the dragon of old, the Devil, Satan who in the last days manifests himself in a man and empire. Isaiah speaks about this battle.

DRAGON'S SECOND FALL

Isa 14:12 KJV) How art thou fallen from heaven, O Lucifer, son of the morning! *how* art thou cut down to the ground, which didst weaken the nations!:13 For thou hast said in thine heart, I will ascend into heaven, I will exalt my throne above the stars of God: I will sit also upon the mount of the congregation, in the sides of the north:14 I will ascend above the heights of the clouds; I will be like the most High.:15 Yet thou shalt be brought down to hell, to the sides of the pit.:16 They that see thee shall narrowly look upon thee, *and* consider thee, *saying, Is* this the man that made the earth to tremble, that did shake kingdoms:17 *That* made the world as a wilderness, and destroyed the cities thereof; *that* opened not the house of his prisoners?:18 All the kings of the nations, *even* all of them, lie in glory, every one in his own house.:19 But thou art cast out of thy grave like an abominable branch, *and as* the raiment of those that are slain, thrust through with a sword, that go down to the stones of the pit; as a carcase trodden under feet.:20 Thou shalt not be joined with them in burial, because thou hast destroyed thy land, *and* slain thy people: the seed of evildoers shall never be renowned.

Notice here he is "cut down" -- a term used for warfare. In Ezekiel's vision he was cast. He was cast down before, because iniquity was found in him. (Ezek 28:15) Here he says I will ascend into heaven and exalt my throne. Isa 14v20 also gives us some important details. He will not join them in the burial.

(Rev 19:20 KJV) And the beast was taken, and with him the false prophet that wrought miracles before him, with which he deceived them that had received the mark of the beast, and them that worshipped his image. These both were cast alive into a lake of fire burning with brimstone.:21 And the remnant were slain with the sword of him that sat upon the horse, which *sword* proceeded out of his mouth: and all the fowls were filled with their flesh.20:1 And I saw an angel come down from heaven, having the key of the bottomless pit and a great chain in his hand. :2 And he laid hold on the dragon, that old serpent, which is the Devil, and Satan, and bound him a thousand years,

When this battle takes place is not given. Neither is his original fall. We are told here he has lost a great advantage. His ability to day and night accuse the brethren as in the book of Job1:6-12, Job2:1-7, Zech 3:12, Zech12:11. His ability to accuse the saints is finished.

The beast is outraged.
The word of God states this is the event that incites the dragon to persecute the woman (Jews represented by 144,000 evangelist) and the remnant of her seeds. The word remnant is "loipoy" meaning those remaining. (remaining Christians.) These are those that after the resurrection of the church (rapture) receive Christ.

Events that happen on earth sometimes have a spiritual significance:
(Dan 11:30 KJV) For the ships of Chittim shall come against him: therefore he shall be grieved, and return, and have indignation against the holy covenant: so shall he do; he shall even return, and have intelligence with them that forsake the holy covenant.

(Dan 11:31 KJV) And arms shall stand on his part, and they shall pollute the sanctuary of strength, and shall take away the daily *sacrifice,* and they shall place the abomination that maketh desolate.:32 And such as do wickedly against the covenant shall he corrupt by flatteries: but the people that do know their God shall be strong, and do *exploits*.

The ships of Cyprus. *(chittim)* This defeat the bible tells us sends him into a rage to break covenant, defile sanctuary and begin persecution of God's redeemed

(Num 24:23-24 KJV) And he took up his parable, and said, Alas, who shall live when God doeth this! :24   And ships *shall come* from the coast of Chittim, and shall afflict Asshur, and shall afflict Eber, and he also shall perish for ever.

Balam gave this unusual prophecy. Dan. Ch11 gives us the rest of the details surrounding the abomination.

(Dan 11:32 KJV) And such as do wickedly against the covenant shall he corrupt by flatteries: but the people that do know their God shall be strong, and do *exploits*

Remember Daniel is receiving revelation concerning "His people". Two groups of Jews are mentioned here: 1st those who know their God and 2nd those people who understand. The second group sides with antichrist or are slain. The 1st group is never mentioned again. Rev 12:14. Remember the word "knew" denotes intimacy. Jerm 2:3 says pastors knew me not. Matt 7:23 says the people who were laboring for Christ but did not know him did not enter in. Let's see the fullness of his defeat.

SAINTS IN HEAVEN

(Rev 12:10 KJV) And I heard a loud voice saying in heaven, Now is come salvation, and strength, and the kingdom of our God, and the power of his Christ: for the accuser of our brethren is cast down, which accused them before our God day and night.

God's rule and authority, The Kingdom of God has come. (Mth. 12:28) The power of his Christ is the preaching of the Gospel. *1Cor1:18, Rm.1:16.*
The part I desire to focus on is "they overcame."

(Rom 16:20 KJV) And the God of peace shall bruise Satan under your feet shortly. The grace of our Lord Jesus Christ *be* with you. Amen.

(1 John 5:4 KJV) For whatsoever is born of God overcometh the world: and this is the victory that overcometh the world, *even* our faith.

(Rev 3:20 KJV) Behold, I stand at the door, and knock: if any man hear my voice, and open the door, I will come in to him, and will sup with him, and he with me.:21 To him that overcometh will I grant to sit with me in my throne, even as I also overcame, and am set down with my Father in his throne.

Jesus is on the thrown Heb 12:2 & Rev 4:2. They overcame is past tense. They (Group, entirety) over came. Nikap is the Greek word for conquered, meaning prevail and victory. This verse John connects with Satan's defeat. Who are they? The first Disciples? First century church? The martyrs? **We see saints in heaven before the tribulation starts.**

(Rev 5:2 KJV) And I saw a strong angel proclaiming with a loud voice, Who is worthy to open the book, and to loose the seals thereof? :3 And no man in heaven, nor in earth, neither under the earth, was able to open the book, neither to look thereon.:4 And I wept much, because no man was found worthy to open and to read the book, neither to look thereon.

Matt 19:28 & Luke 27:30. No error men in heaven

Rev 5:9 KJV) And they sung a new song, saying, Thou art worthy to take the book, and to open the seals thereof: for thou wast slain, and hast redeemed us to God by thy blood out of every kindred, and tongue, and people, and nation;

(Rev 5:10 KJV) And hast made us unto our God kings and priests: and we shall reign on the earth.
(Rev 5:11 KJV) And I beheld, and I heard the voice of many angels round about the throne and the beasts and the elders: and the number of them was ten thousand times ten thousand, and thousands of thousands;

The word "angels" is the same used in chapter one to describe leaders of the church, note they are around about the throne. The bible is very clear. They are the redeemed of Christ from every race and nation on the earth. (1Peter 2:9 & Ex 19:6) They are awaiting the final pages of prophecy to be loosed, the Seals to be broken, the judgments to come. In verse 10 they proclaim they shall reign on the earth with Christ.

(2 Tim 2:12 KJV) If we suffer, we shall also reign with *him:* if we deny *him,* he also will deny us:
(Rev 20:6 KJV) Blessed and holy *is* he that hath part in the first resurrection: on such the second death hath no power, but they shall be priests of God and of Christ, and shall reign with him a thousand years.

(Job 19:25 KJV) For I know *that* my redeemer liveth, and *that* he shall stand at the latter *day* upon the earth:26 And *though* after my skin *worms* destroy this *body,* yet in my flesh shall I see God:27 Whom I shall see for myself, and mine eyes shall behold, and not another; *though* my reins be consumed within me.

The bible is clear. The 1st resurrection saints will reign in millennium. It's also important to note this is a **Christian and Jewish resurrection**, Old Testament saints, together with the church, the redeemed of God. (Hebrew 11v 39-40)

(Exo 19:5-6 KJV) Now therefore, if ye will obey my voice indeed, and keep my covenant, then ye shall be a peculiar treasure unto me above all people: for all the earth *is* mine: {6} And ye shall be unto me a kingdom of priests, and an holy nation. These *are* the words which thou shalt speak unto the children of Israel.

(1 Pet 2:9-10 KJV) But ye *are* a chosen generation, a royal priesthood, an holy nation, a peculiar people; that ye should show forth the praises of him who hath called you out of darkness into his marvellous light: *{10}* Which in time past *were* not a people, but *are* now the people of God: which had not obtained mercy, but now have obtained mercy.

Michael the Archangel is mentioned in Jude 9 and 1Thess. ch 4. He is a special angel "chief princes". Dan10:13 & 21. Also called prince of the Jewish people. We see Michael in warfare near the tribulation period. Paul gives us insight. 1st Thess.4:16-17, is an all Christian resurrection.(In Christ) You will find the Archangel very involved in resurrections.

1Corth 15:51-52 Paul stops and mentions the mystery of resurrection. This too is strictly a Christian resurrection as also Matt 24:39-41 *(it's unlikely those with the mark & without will be together nor fields or produce)*
Paul as in 1st Thessalonians mentions the final trumpet. This is not to be confused with the seven trumpet judgments. Jesus, the key to prophecy, tells us in Matt 24:31 at his coming a trumpet will be sounded to gather the elect. These are the tribulation saints at a dual resurrection, not the church. *(Which Paul declares is the last trump)* The last trumpet Paul spoke of is before the Great Tribulation begins. (Also Rev ch12v11-12) (see Rev 11v15-18) Paul refers to trumpets of deliverance. *(This trumpet is possibly a declaration of the completion of the church era)* The pattern in all the resurrections is deliverance before judgment. Interesting note: the deliverance of Lot & Noah were not only before judgment but also unnoticed.

Rev. Chapter 12 ends with the woman escaping. Those who know their God escape in Dan11. I believe this to be the

144,000. What we know for sure is the Beast sends floods, which symbolizes armies of troops. The earth helps her (Num.16:32) and God supernaturally assists her on eagle wings. (Exodus 19:4)
The events are now in Israel as he assaults the believers in Jesus Christ. Rev. 12:17 & Rev.13:7-8

(Zec 12:10 KJV) And I will pour upon the house of David, and upon the inhabitants of Jerusalem, the spirit of grace and of supplications: and they shall look upon me whom they have pierced, and they shall mourn for him, as one mourneth for *his* only *son,* and shall be in bitterness for him, as one that is in bitterness for *his* firstborn.
(Zec 12:11 KJV) In that day shall there be a great mourning in Jerusalem, as the mourning of Hadadrimmon in the valley of Megiddon.
(Zec 12:12 KJV) And the land shall mourn, every family apart; the family of the house of David apart, and their wives apart; the family of the house of Nathan apart, and their wives apart;
(Zec 12:13 KJV) The family of the house of Levi apart, and their wives apart; the family of Shimei apart, and their wives apart;
(Zec 12:14 KJV) All the families that remain, every family apart, and their wives apart.

Dan tells us those who understand this event will instruct many, but will be martyred. (Dan11:35)

(Jer 6:23 KJV) They shall lay hold on bow and spear; they *are* cruel, and have no mercy; their voice roareth like the sea; and they ride upon horses, set in array as men for war against thee, O daughter of Zion.
(Jer 6:24 KJV) We have heard the fame thereof: our hands wax feeble: anguish hath taken hold of us, *and* pain, as of a woman in travail.
(Jer 6:25 KJV) Go not forth into the field, nor walk by the way; for the sword of the enemy *and* fear *is* on every side.
(Jer 6:26 KJV) O daughter of my people, gird *thee* with sackcloth, and wallow thyself in ashes: make thee mourning, *as for* an only son, most bitter lamentation: for the spoiler shall suddenly come upon us.
Matt 24:17-18.

16
The Harlot

(Rev 17:5-7 KJV) And upon her forehead *was* a name written, MYSTERY, BABYLON THE GREAT, THE MOTHER OF HARLOTS AND ABOMINATIONS OF THE EARTH. *{6}* And I saw the woman drunken with the blood of the saints, and with the blood of the martyrs of Jesus: and when I saw her, I wondered with great admiration. *{7}* And the angel said unto me, Wherefore didst thou marvel? I will tell thee the mystery of the woman, and of the beast that carrieth her, which hath the seven heads and ten horns.

Mystery Babylon the Mother of Harlots began in Gen ch11 at the tower of Babel. **It is the first recorded false religion that sought to unite all mankind under the one banner, self-glory**. (Gen 11v4) This is the basis of all false religion, to divert trust in the true and the living God and trust in mans ability. Though God scattered the people, the tenets of this religion have survived history and we see a reemergence of her global influence in the latter days.

Rev17v.5 & Rev 17v18 tells us it is a "**city**" That reigns over Kings of Earth. She is carried by the beast of the revised Roman Empire and She (*The city*) sits on seven mountains. (Rev.17v9) Commentators debate whether this is Babylon or Rome. Another hint is she's drunk with blood of the martyrs of Jesus Christ. A study of the religion of ancient Babylon revealed this:

Temples and chapels dedicated to one deity or another; Babylon, for example , possessed more than 50 temples in Chaldean times (8th to 6th century BC). Temples services were generally conducted in open courts containing fountains for ablution and altars for sacrifices. The cella, or inner part of the temple, in which the statue of the deity stood on a pedestal in a special niche, was the holy of holies, and only the high priest and other privileged members of the clergy and court were permitted to enter it. In the temple complexes of the larger cities, a ziggurat, or staged tower, was often built, crowned by a small sanctuary, which probably was reserved for the all-important sacred – marriage ceremony celebrated in connection with the new – year festival. The up keep of the major Babylonian temples require large revenues, which were provided primarily by gifts and endowments from the court and the wealthy. In the course of the centuries, some of the major Babylonian temples accumulated immense wealth and came into possession of large estates and factories employing large numbers of serfs and slaves. Primarily, however, The temple was the house of God, in which all the needs of the deity were provided for in accordance with ancient rites and impressive ceremonies carried out by a vast institutionalized clergy. The latter comprised high priests, sacrifice priests, musicians, singers, magicians, soothsayers, diviners, dream interpreters, astrologers, female devotees, and hierodules (temple slaves).

Sacrifices, which were offered daily, consisted of animal and vegetable foods, libations of water, wine, and beer, and the burning of incense. Numerous annual and monthly festivals were held, including a feast to celebrate the new moon. The most important festival of all was the new year at the spring equinox; it was known as the Akitu festival because some of its more esoteric ritual was enacted in Akitu, Marduk's shrine outside of Babylon. The festival lasted 11 days and included such rites as purification, sacrifice, propitiation, penance, and absolution, but it also involved colorful processions. The culmination was probably the sacred – marriage ceremony previously mentioned, which took place in the sanctuary crowning the ziggurat Beliefs
Babylonian documents indicate that the ethical and moral beliefs of the people stressed goodness and truth, law and order, justice and freedom, wisdom and learning, and courage and loyalty. Mercy and compassion were espoused, and special protection was accorded widows, orphans, refugees, the poor, and the oppressed. Immoral and unethical acts were considered transgressions against the Gods and the divine order and were believed to be punished by the gods accordingly. No one was considered without sin, and therefore all suffering was held to be deserved. The proper course for Babylonians unhappy with their condition in life was not to argue and complain but to plead and wail, to lament and confess their inevitable sins and failings before their personal god, who acted as their mediator in the assembly of the great gods.
.(Encarta Encyclopedia 1998 version.)

THE IDENTITY

The World is dominated with religions that are very similar to this Babylonian model of Idol (statue) worship. Erection of specialized temple for certain rites and ceremonies, special rites for purification, penance and absolution by priests, wailing and lamenting for personal favor from a deity are common traits of religions worldwide.

(Rev 17:1 KJV) And there came one of the seven angels which had the seven vials, and talked with me, saying unto me, Come hither; I will show unto thee the judgment of the great whore that sitteth upon many waters: :15 And he saith unto me, The waters which thou sawest, where the whore sitteth, are peoples, and multitudes, and nations, and tongues.

Only one church in Europe has crossed racial barriers, languages and has branches around the world. Only one has influence with Governments around the world.

(Rev 17:9 KJV) And here *is* the mind which hath wisdom. The seven heads are seven mountains, on which the woman sitteth.

Only one worldwide religion has its headquarters with a city on seven hills. Those hills are Capitoline, Quirinal, Viminal, Esquitine, Caelian. Aventurine and Palatine that make up the city limit boundaries of Rome. Idols are not part of Christian worship, neither is praying to dead saints. Isa 8v19-20. Yet the Babylonians had a God for every occasion, travel, athletics etc. -- over 5000 in all.

(Rev 18:9-10 KJV) And the kings of the earth, who have committed fornication and lived deliciously with her, shall bewail her, and lament for her, when they shall see the smoke of her burning, {10} Standing afar off for the fear of her torment, saying, Alas, alas that great city Babylon, that mighty city! for in one hour is thy judgment come.

The mystery religion has practices that identify with most religions and are easily adapted. That's why she is the **Mother of Harlots**. What makes her unique is she is identified as being Christian. This is why fornication is implied -- mixing the truth of God's word with pagan practices. To practice such things is sin in the eyes of God. Only one religious institution in Western Europe fits the description of Rev.17. Christians have one mediator. (1Tim2v5) No priest or Pope can regulate God's forgiveness for the dead nor mediate between God and man. Christian worship doesn't revolve around temples. Acts17v24 & 1Cor3v16. In Babylonian worship the temple and religious buildings were believed to house the presence of God. The building in itself became an Image *(Idol)* a focus of worship. Indulgences *(paying for the sins of the dead)* doing penance, wailing and lamenting *(self induced suffering for favor)* is not only non-Christian but an insult to the blood of Jesus Christ! Hundreds of thousands of Protestant Christians were murdered during the reign of the Popes. *Ref (Ralph Woodrow Babylon Mystery Religion.)*

The greatest concern is that she is a harlot. There is no faithfulness found to the true and living God but to many false Gods. The word of God spends two chapters to ensure she is properly identified. God's opinion of her is made very clear along with her judgment. This seems to be a major issue concerning the judgment of God and we have this warning.

(Rev 18:4-5 KJV) And I heard another voice from heaven, saying, Come out of her, my people, that ye be not partakers of her sins, and that ye receive not of her plagues. *{5}* For her sins have reached unto heaven, and God hath remembered her iniquities

95

17
THE ELECT

IDENTITY IN SCRIPTURE
Books of prophecy have been built on this one issue.
This group is called the Elect of God. The bible is very clear
who the Elect are. They are the redeemed of God. The word in
both New and Old Testament means favorite or chosen. Here
are some examples from scripture.

THE ELECT IN THE BIBLE

Prophecy of Jesus

(Isa 42:1 KJV) Behold my servant, whom I uphold; mine elect, *in whom*
my soul delighted; I have put my spirit upon him: he shall bring forth
judgment to the Gentiles.
(1 Pet 2:6 KJV) Wherefore also it is contained in the scripture, Behold, I
lay in Sion a chief corner stone, elect, precious: and he that believeth on
him shall not be confounded.

Israel

(Isa 45:4 KJV) For Jacob my servant's sake, and Israel mine elect, I have
even called thee by thy name: I have surnamed thee, though thou hast not
known me.

People of the millennial kingdom

(Isa 65:20-22 KJV) There shall be no more thence an infant of days, nor
an old man that hath not filled his days: for the child shall die an hundred
years old; but the sinner *being* an hundred years old shall be accursed.
{21} And they shall build houses, and inhabit *them;* and they shall plant

vineyards, and eat the fruit of them. {22} They shall not build, and another inhabit; they shall not plant, and another eat: for as the days of a tree *are* the days of my people, and mine elect shall long enjoy the work of their hands.

This is concerning believers

(Rom 8:32-34 KJV) He that spared not his own Son, but delivered him up for us all, how shall he not with him also freely give us all things? {33} Who shall lay any thing to the charge of God's elect? *It is* God that justifieth. {34} Who *is* he that condemneth? *It is* Christ that died, yea rather, that is risen again, who is even at the right hand of God, who also maketh intercession for us.

(.also see 1Pet 1v2,Titus1v1,Col3v12,Lk18v7.)

THE REAL QUESTION…
We can see the Elect are the redeemed, the Jew first then the Gentile. The true question is, who are **the resurrected elect referred to in Math 24 v31?** To understand whom the Lord is referring to, you must have the bigger picture.

144,000. LIVE THROUGH THE TRIBULATION
Lets look at the order of earth's final days, as we know it. The bible is very clear that the millennium kingdom begins after the final judgment.

(Rev 19:20-21 KJV) And the beast was taken, and with him the false prophet that wrought miracles before him, with which he deceived them that had received the mark of the beast, and them that worshipped his image. These both were cast alive into a lake of fire burning with brimstone. {21} And the remnant were slain with the sword of him that sat upon the horse, which *sword* proceeded out of his mouth: and all the fowls were filled with their flesh.
(Rev 20:1-2 KJV) And I saw an angel come down from heaven, having the key of the bottomless pit and a great chain in his hand. {2} And he laid

hold on the dragon, that old serpent, which is the Devil, and Satan, **and bound him a thousand years,**

They're survivors. There's the Jewish remnant that escape through the slit in the Mount of Olives *(Zech14v5)* during Armageddon. The beginning mark of the Millennium reign is the final judgment on the beast and his followers. Near the end of the millennium we see the earth repopulated.

Rev 20:7 And when the thousand years are expired, Satan shall be loosed out of his prison,:8 And shall go out to deceive the nations which are in the four quarters of the earth, Gog and Magog, to gather them together to battle: the number of whom is as the sand of the sea.Hear Isa prophecy on this time period.

(Isa 66:20-24 KJV) And they shall bring all your brethren *for* an offering unto the LORD out of all nations upon horses, and in chariots, and in litters, and upon mules, and upon swift beasts, to my holy mountain Jerusalem, saith the LORD, as the children of Israel bring an offering in a clean vessel into the house of the LORD. *{21}* And I will also take of them for priests *and* for Levites, saith the LORD. *{22}* For as the new heavens and the new earth, which I will make, shall remain before me, saith the LORD, so shall your seed and your name remain. *{23}* And it shall come to pass, *that* from one new moon to another, and from one sabbath to another, shall all flesh come to worship before me, saith the LORD. *{24}* And they shall go forth, and look upon the carcasses of the men that have transgressed against me: for their worm shall not die, neither shall their fire be quenched; and they shall be an abhorring unto all flesh.

After their witness to the gentile nations we see the 144,000 Jews returning to Jerusalem from the nations after the judgment of the world's armies.

RESURRECTION OF THE DEAD

We also find another key in Dan ch12v10-11. The angel tells Daniel the defiling of temple will last 31/2 years. Then he adds blessed is he who waits 45 more days. They're people waiting. Dan12v1-2 gives more information. The last verse in Dan.chpt.11 ends with the beast in the battle of Armageddon. Right at this point Daniel is told.

(Dan 12:1-2 KJV) And at that time shall Michael stand up, the great prince which standeth for the children of thy people: and there shall be a time of trouble, such as never was since there was a nation *even* to that same time: and at that time thy people shall be delivered, every one that shall be found written in the book. *{2}* And many of them that sleep in the dust of the earth shall awake, some to everlasting life, and some to shame *and* everlasting contempt.

Daniel prophecy is concerning the Jews.
The word delivered does not imply resurrection. The hebrew word is "Malat"it means released, rescued ,delivered or escape.
<u>Daniels account shows the living delivered and two groups of dead awaken</u>. One group experiences life --the other shame. This is in perfect agreement with John's vision in revelation.

(Rev 14:14-16 KJV) And I looked, and behold a white cloud, and upon the cloud *one* sat like unto the Son of man, having on his head a golden crown, and in his hand a sharp sickle. *{15}* And another angel came out of the temple, crying with a loud voice to him that sat on the cloud, Thrust in thy sickle, and reap: for the time is come for thee to reap; for the harvest of the earth is ripe. *{16}* And he that sat on the cloud thrust in his sickle on the earth; and the earth was reaped.   Awake to life. *(Rev19v20 also confirms this.)*

(Rev 14:17-19 KJV) And another angel came out of the temple which is in heaven, he also having a sharp sickle. *{18}* And another angel came out from the altar, which had
power over fire; and cried with a loud cry to him that had the sharp sickle, saying, Thrust in thy sharp sickle, and gather the clusters of the vine of the earth; for her grapes are fully ripe. *{19}* And the angel thrust in his sickle into the earth, and gathered the vine of the earth, and cast *it* into the great winepress of the wrath of God. Awake to death

99

The winepress is made clear

Rev 14:10 KJV) The same shall drink of the wine of the wrath of God, which is poured out without mixture into the cup of his indignation; and he shall be tormented with fire and brimstone in the presence of the holy angels, and in the presence of the Lamb:
These are those who followed the beast.

Jesus also confirms this truth in the parable of the wheat and the tares. The angels separate the righteous from the children of the wicked. This pattern is also found in parable of the sheep and goats.

Who are these that awake to life? Who are these that Jesus gathers from the four corners of the earth? I will let the scriptures speak.

These are the Elect of Math.24v31

(Rev 7:9KJV) {9} After this I beheld, and, lo, a great multitude, which no man could number, of all nations, and kindreds, and people, and tongues, stood before the throne, and before the Lamb, clothed with white robes, and palms in their hands;

(Rev 15:2-3 KJV) And I saw as it were a sea of glass mingled with fire: and them that had gotten the victory over the beast, and over his image, and over his mark, *and* over the number of his name, stand on the sea of glass, having the harps of God. {3} And they sing the song of Moses the servant of God, and the song of the Lamb, saying, Great and marvellous *are* thy works, Lord God Almighty; just and true *are* thy ways, thou King of saints.

(Rev 6:9-10 KJV) And when he had opened the fifth seal, I saw under the altar the souls of them that were slain for the word of God, and for the testimony which they held: *{10}* And they cried with a loud voice, saying,

How long, O Lord, holy and true, dost thou not judge and avenge our blood on them that dwell on the earth?

:11 And white robes were given unto every one of them; and it was said unto them, that they should rest yet for a little season, until their fellowservants also and their brethren, that should be killed as they *were,* should be fulfilled.

(Rev 20:4 KJV) And I saw thrones, and they sat upon them, and judgment was given unto them: and *I saw* the souls of them that were beheaded for the witness of Jesus, and for the word of God, and which had not worshipped the beast, neither his image, neither had received *his* mark upon their foreheads, or in their hands; and they lived and reigned with Christ a thousand years

(Mat 24:31 KJV) And he shall send his angels with a great sound of a trumpet, and they shall gather together his elect from the four winds, from one end of heaven to the other.

THE ELECT ARE THOSE KILLED FOR THEIR FAITH DURING THE GREAT TRIBULATION.

PART 4.
PUTTING IT ALL
TOGETHER

If you run yesterday's soft ware with today's computer
You're bound to have problems. (Math 9:17)

QUESTIONS TO PONDER.

1.   Is our God a God of order?
2.   If so what order is the book of
     Revelation?
3.   Where do we find a confirmation of
     that order in scripture?

18
THE
MYSTERY
OF
TRIUNE PROPHECY

Have you ever thought after reading the book of Revelation you were looking at a jigsaw puzzle -- uncertain how and where all the pieces fit? I believe this information will help your understanding.

In Gen.Chpt.40 & 41 a powerful lesson is given on the subject of interpretation. Joseph has interpreted several dreams (visions). One was for a butler in which three branches were seen. Joseph interprets each branch as a separate time frame of one day. The object, which is a branch in this case, held a specific meaning for the one to whom the interpretation was directed. The branch contained the fruit of the vine by which the butler at the end of vision serves his master. Joseph gives a similar interpretation to the baker. The objects again represent time frames, white baskets. Their relation to the baker involves his job, his head and his flesh being eaten.

I want to point out a pattern of interpretation because patterns are consistent in the word of God. Joseph gives another interpretation for Pharaoh. Though more complex the same rules of interpretation are used. Seven fat cows and seven gaunt represent separate time frames. Each is one year for a total of fourteen years. Their relationship to Pharaoh was the pastoral condition of his kingdom. Seven plump heads of grain and seven thin heads of grain. Each a separate time frame, equal fourteen years representing his kingdoms agricultural state. Listen to Joseph's interpretation in Gen 41:26-28 KJV. The seven good kine *are* seven years; and the seven good ears *are* seven years: the dream *is* one. *{27}* And the seven thin and ill favoured kine that came up after them *are* seven years; and the seven empty ears blasted with the east wind shall be seven years of famine. *{28}* This *is* the thing which I have spoken unto Pharaoh: What God *is* about to do he showeth unto Pharaoh.

They are one, meaning both dreams of separate objects are the same time frame. He does not interpret them one after another but side by side.

	1ST DREAM		2ND DREAM		
TIME FRAME IN ONE YEAR	COW	|	WHEAT =	CONDITIONS	
IN ONE YEAR	COW	|	WHEAT =	CONDITIONS	
	E.C.T......		E.C.T..................		

In the book of Revelation John has a vision of seven Seals then seven Trumpets and afterwards seven Vials. Many in the past have interpreted them one after another, twenty-one separate time frames. I believe they are one!

There are seven time frames and three objects. Each object points to a specific issue and event in that time frame. I call it Triune Prophecy.

SEAL | TRUMPET | VIAL = EACH ONE THE SAME TIME FRAME

Some one once said the Book of Revelation is not in any set order. That's not true. The series of Judgments are in perfect order. The mystery is the three Judgments (Seal, Trumpets Vials) are one .We know this because we find the same events in all three. If they where separate, events like The Day of The Lord would be happening several times. What we see in the judgments are three different perspectives of the same Judgment. The Seals give a view from heaven, the Vials from earth and the Trumpets mediate.

LETS LOOK AT THE CONNECTION

7th Seal

(Rev 8:1 KJV) And when he had opened the seventh seal, there was silence in heaven about the space of half an hour.
(Rev 8:5 KJV) And the angel took the censer, and filled it with fire of the altar, and cast *it* into the earth: and there were voices, and thunderings, and lightnings, and an earthquake.

7th Trumpet

(Rev 11:15 KJV) And the seventh angel sounded; and there were great voices in heaven, saying, The kingdoms of this world are become *the kingdoms* of our Lord, and of his Christ; and he shall reign for ever and ever.
(Rev 11:19 KJV) And the temple of God was opened in heaven, and there was seen in his temple the ark of his testament: and there were lightnings, and voices, and thunderings, and an earthquake, and great hail.

7th Vial

(Rev 16:16-18 KJV) And he gathered them together into a place called in the Hebrew tongue Armageddon. {17} And the seventh angel poured out his vial into the air; and there came a great voice out of the temple of heaven, from the throne, saying, It is done. {18} And there were voices, and thunders, and lightnings; and there was a great earthquake, such as was not since men were upon the earth, so mighty an earthquake, *and* so great.

The Earth Quakes are specific. The events in each are the same. The event of this earthquake is central in bible prophecy. What we're seeing is the conclusion of the Day of the Lord.

The Day of the Lord. Joel 3:15-17 & Zech 14:1-5

(Joel 3:14-17 KJV) Multitudes, multitudes in the valley of decision: for the day of the LORD *is* near in the valley of decision. {15} The sun and the moon shall be darkened, and the stars shall withdraw their shining. {16} The LORD also shall roar out of Zion, and utter his voice from Jerusalem; and the heavens and the earth shall shake: but the LORD *will be* the hope of his people, and the strength of the children of Israel. {17} So shall ye know that I *am* the LORD your God dwelling in Zion, my holy mountain: then shall Jerusalem be holy, and there shall no strangers pass through her any more.
.(see Day of the Lord)

(Acts 2:16 KJV) But this is that which was spoken by the prophet Joel; (Acts 2:19-20 KJV) And I will show wonders in heaven above, and signs in the earth beneath; blood, and fire, and vapour of smoke: {20} The sun shall be turned into darkness, and the moon into blood, before that great and notable day of the Lord come:

(Mat 24:29 KJV) Immediately after the tribulation of those days shall the sun be darkened, and the moon shall not give her light, and the stars shall fall from heaven, and the powers of the heavens shall be shaken:

The signs we see after the 6th Seal, the sun darkened and moon to blood, are The Day of The Lord. (Rev6v12-13)

Fire is also part of the final Judgment. Rev19:2 Rev14v14-20,v18-19,v10-11, Jesus speaks this. Matt 25:41, Matt 5:22 & Luke 12:5. These are all the same judgments that fall in sequence.

WHY THE NAMES

The three are one and yet they are separate. (1 John 5:7 KJV) For there are three that bear record in heaven, **the Father, the Word, and the Holy Ghost**: and these three are one.

The symbols here are important.

1). " The Seal" as we know is a symbol of authority. In ancient times a letter written with the king's seal could not be reversed. (Ester 8:8)

The seal identifies and it means preserved and kept secure. No one in heaven could break them open. (Rev 5:2 KJV)

The seal represents the authority of all mighty God. " The Father" Jesus said no one knows the time or season but the Father. Acts1v7, Matt 24:36.

2.) " The Trumpet" words of warning, (Jerm.4:19 & Ezek 33:4) Declaration (Nehm 4:20) Gathering (Number 10:4). Human voice or word *Exodus 19:16

(Rev 1:10 KJV) I was in the Spirit on the Lord's day, and heard behind me a great voice, as of a trumpet,(:11) Saying, I am Alpha and Omega, the first and the last: and, What thou seest, write in a book, and send it unto the seven churches which are in Asia; unto Ephesus, and unto Smyrna, and unto Pergamos, and unto Thyatira, and unto Sardis, and unto Philadelphia, and unto Laodicea. (SEE ALSO JOHN CHPT.1)

The Trumpet is The Word.

3.) " The Vial" (shallow cup) . I Sam10:1 It contained the anointing oil. The word "Vials" or golden Vials Should not be confused with the Judgments. (Rev5v8) They contained the

Odours, (*Ex30v35 ingredients for holy incense*) which are symbolic of prayers of the saints.

Its also important to note **all the prayers** where sacrifice on the golden altar and should not be confused with the wrath of God poured from the Vial Judgments. (Rev15v7) Oil is a symbol of the <u>Holy Ghost.</u> (Note : John informs us in his gospel that Judgment is also carried out by Holy Spirit.)

What we see in the judgments is the order of Heaven.
The seal: is the sovereign will of God, Where all things begin and originate. Matt 24:36 & 20:23, Rev 4:11.

The trumpet is the word. John tells us John 1:1-4, all things were made by Him. He's the Word, the creator. The Word, which is God, initiates the will of God and creates.

The Vial: The Holy Ghost. He is the power by which the word of God is accomplished on earth.

(Acts 1:8 KJV) But ye shall receive power, after that the Holy Ghost is come upon you: and ye shall be witnesses unto me both in Jerusalem, and in all Judaea, and in Samaria, and unto the uttermost part of the earth. John 16:13, Gen 1:2, 1Cor 6:14, Acts 1:8 Rom15:18-19 The Lord depart that the Spirit might come John 16:7 & Rev 22:17.

Example Third Judgement:

3 Seal	3 Trumpet	3 Vial
Command is famine.	famine Created	The results on earth.
Rev 6:5	8v10	16v4

We see this in the book of Genesis chapter 1:3-4. God's will, Gods will spoken and Gods will created.

(Gen 1:6 KJV) **And God said**, Let there be a firmament in the midst of the waters, and let it divide the waters from the waters.(:7) **And God made** the firmament, and divided the waters which *were* under the firmament from the waters which *were* above the firmament: **and it was so.**

We see here the workmanship of the Trinity. "Note" God <u>said</u> and God <u>made.</u> There is a very close relationship between the word & spirit of God.

(2 Sam 23:2) The spirit of the LORD spake by me, and his word *was* in my tongue.   Isa 59:21, Zech 4:6,
(Mat 22:29) Jesus answered and said unto them, Ye do err, not knowing the scriptures, nor the power of God
(2 Pet 1:21)   For the prophecy came not in old time by the will of man: but holy men of God spake *as they were* moved by the Holy Ghost. .
(Other examples...Luke 12:12, John 3:34, Acts 10:37-38, *Eph 1:13, & 6:17, Heb 6:4-5)

As you study you will find a close relationship between the Trumpet and Vial Judgments. You will notice that the Vail judgments simply show the results of Gods will on earth as well as its completion. (Rev 21:9 last plagues) It's also important to understand John's describing events to the best of his ability. "Great star from Heaven" could be a meteor or a nuclear weapon. Whatever the description we see the results of its power." Note" in Genesis there is no time factor given between spoken will and creation. The last plagues are the final results of God's will. Example

3rd   Seal –   Famine: God's will
            Trumpet – Star Wormwood fall **1\3**
                        water to Blood
            Vail – The end or conclusion to God's
                  will. **All** the water to blood.

2nd   Seal – No Peace ,War

God's will
Trumpet – 1st strike 1\3 ships sea life
Destroyed. 1\3 sea to blood.
Vail – Conclusion of War: all sea like
Blood of dead men.

There are some important details in the judgment.
The last three are unlike the first four. John in Rev.chpt.6 is told
to view each Seal being open by one of the four beasts. First the
lion, then Ox, Man & Eagle. John is not told to come and see
the last three. We find in the trumpet judgment that these final
three are **woe judgments** Rev 8:13. It's also important to
separate judgments from other events.

Armageddon initiates the 6th judgment. The Day of the Lord is
part of the 6th judgment and ends with the 7th. The Second
Coming begins after the 6th and concludes with establishing of
physical kingdom on earth. (Rev 11:13 & 7:1) The 7th judgment is
not part of the tribulations of the earth. Jesus reveals the
tribulation over before it begins. (Math24v29) The 7th judgment is
God's completion. In seven judgments he shall purged the
earth.   (See Last Judgment pg.111)

(Rev 11:18 KJV) And the nations were angry, and thy wrath is come,
and the time of the dead, that they should be judged, and that thou
shouldest give reward unto thy servants the prophets, and to the saints, and
them that fear thy name, small and great; and shouldest destroy them
which destroy the earth .also Isa 24:19-21

THE MYSTERY OF TRIUNE PROPHECY

SEAL GODS WILL	TRUMPET CREATION	VIAL RESULTS
1ST JUDGEMENT CONQUER GOES FORTH	1/3 OF EARTH VEGITATION DESTROYED BY FIRE	PESTILENCE ON BEAST KDM.
2ND JUDGEMENT WAR GOES FORTH	WAR CREATED 1/3 SEALIFE AND SHIPS DESTROYED ,.SEA TO BLOOD	WARS END ALL IN SEA DIE . SEA, BLOOD OF DEAD MAN
3RD JUDGEMENT FAMINE GOES FORTH	FAMINE CREATED 1/3 FRESH WATER POISONED	FAMINES END ALL WA. POISONED
4TH JUDGEMENT DEATH AND HELL GOES FORTH	D&H CREATED 1/3 LIGHT SMITTEN	DEATH ,HELL END MEN SCORTCH BY SUN

THE THREE WOE JUDGEMENTS
these John was not called to see.

5TH 1ST WOE MARTYERS REVEALED	LOCUSTS RELEASED FROM PIT	LOCUSTS ATTACKS BEAST KINGDOM
6TH 2ND WOE- DAY OF THE LORD REVEALED-ARMAGEDDON	WAR BEGINS 1/3 HUMANITY KILLED	EUPRA.DRIES AND KGS EST. COME (Winepress of Gods Wrath) (Nations Destroyed)
7TH 3RD WOE EARTHQUAKE / HAIL FIRE FROM HEAVEN before trumpet jdg. Rev8v5	EARTHQUAKE / HAIL FIRE ON EARTH before vial jdg.Rev14.20 & 10	EARTHQUAKE /HAIL FIRE IN LAKE OF before 1000yr.reighn Rev19v20

There are events we find with several mentions. These are important to see for with out them we don't get a complete picture. I will call these threepeats because they occur three times in the book of revelation.

THREEPEATS

THE SECOND COMING

(Rev 10:1 KJV) And I saw another mighty angel come down from heaven, clothed with a cloud: and a rainbow *was* upon his head, and his face *was* as it were the sun, and his feet as pillars of fire:
(Rev 10:7) But in the days of the voice of the seventh angel, when he shall begin to sound, the mystery of God should be finished, as he hath declared to his servants the prophets.
Coming from Heaven cloth with a cloud.

(Rev 14:14 KJV) And I looked, and behold a white cloud, and upon the cloud *one* sat like unto the Son of man, having on his head a golden crown, and in his hand a sharp sickle.(:15) And another angel came out of the temple, crying with a loud voice to him that sat on the cloud, Thrust in thy sickle, and reap: for the time is come for thee to reap; for the harvest of the earth is ripe.
Coming on a cloud.

(Rev 19:14 KJV) And the armies *which were* in heaven followed him upon white horses, clothed in fine linen, white and clean.(:15) And out of his mouth goeth a sharp sword, that with it he should smite the nations: and he shall rule them with a rod of iron: and he treadeth the winepress of the fierceness and wrath of Almighty God.
(:16) And he hath on *his* vesture and on his thigh a name written, KING OF KINGS, AND LORD OF LORDS.
Gathering with the Saints in Heaven.

TRIBULATION MARTYRS

(Rev 7:9 KJV) After this I beheld, and, lo, a great multitude, which no man could number, of all nations, and kindreds, and people, and tongues, stood before the throne, and before the Lamb, clothed with white robes, and palms in their hands;

(Rev 7:14 KJV) And I said unto him, Sir, thou knowest. And he said to me, These are they which came out of great tribulation, and have washed their robes, and made them white in the blood of the Lamb.

Arrival in Heaven.

(Rev 15:2 KJV) And I saw as it were a sea of glass mingled with fire: and them that had gotten the victory over the beast, and over his image, and over his mark, *and* over the number of his name, stand on the sea of glass, having the harps of God.(:3) And they sing the song of Moses the servant of God, and the song of the Lamb, saying, Great and marvellous *are* thy works, Lord God Almighty; just and true *are* thy ways, thou King of saints.

New Song if you read carefully you'll note. The harps played in previous chapter were not from 144,000 but heaven.

(Rev 20:4 KJV) And I saw thrones, and they sat upon them, and judgment was given unto them: and *I saw* the souls of them that were beheaded for the witness of Jesus, and for the word of God, and which had not worshipped the beast, neither his image, neither had received *his* mark upon their foreheads, or in their hands; and they lived and reigned with Christ a thousand years.

On the Earth, reign with Christ.

NEW JERUSALEM

(Rev 11:19 KJV) And the temple of God was opened in heaven, and there was seen in his temple the ark of his testament: and there were lightnings, and voices, and thunderings, and an earthquake, and great hail.

(Rev 15:5 KJV) And after that I looked, and, behold, the temple of the tabernacle of the testimony in heaven was opened:

Opened up in Heaven.

(Rev 21:1 KJV) And I saw a new heaven and a new earth: for the first heaven and the first earth were passed away; and there was no more sea.
(Rev 21:2 KJV) And I John saw the holy city, new Jerusalem, coming down from God out of heaven, prepared as a bride adorned for her

husband. (Rev 21:3 KJV) And I heard a great voice out of heaven saying, Behold, the tabernacle of God *is* with men, and he will dwell with them, and they shall be his people, and God himself shall be with them, *and be their God.*
Coming down to men.

THE JUDGMENT OF HELL AND FIRE

(2 Pet 3:10 KJV) But the day of the Lord will come as a thief in the night; in the which the heavens shall pass away with a great noise, and the elements shall melt with fervent heat, the earth also and the works that are therein shall be burned up.(11) *Seeing* then *that* all these things shall be dissolved, what manner *of persons* ought ye to be in *all* holy conversation and godliness,(12) Looking for and hasting unto the coming of the day of God, wherein the heavens being on fire shall be dissolved, and the elements shall melt with fervent heat?(13 Nevertheless we, according to his promise, look for new heavens and a new earth, wherein dwelleth righteousness.

1)(Rev 8:5 KJV) And the angel took the censer, and filled it with fire of the altar, and cast *it* into the earth: and there were voices, and thunderings, and lightnings, and an earthquake.
Opening of 7th seal………….. Fire from Heaven

2) (Rev 14:10-11 KJV) The same shall drink of the wine of the wrath of God, which is poured out without mixture into the cup of his indignation; and he shall be tormented with fire and brimstone in the presence of the holy angels, and in the presence of the Lamb::11 And the smoke of their torment ascendeth up for ever and ever: and they have no rest day nor night, who worship the beast and his image, and whosoever receiveth the mark of his name. ……Those that receive the Mark of The Beast…Fire Eternal.

3) (Rev 19:20 KJV) And the beast was taken, and with him the false prophet that wrought miracles before him, with which he deceived them that had received the mark of the beast, and them that worshipped his image. These both were cast alive into a lake of fire burning with brimstone.

(Rev 19:21 KJV) And the remnant were slain with the sword of him that sat upon the horse, which *sword* proceeded out of his mouth: and all the fowls were filled with their flesh. .... Beast and False Prophet in the lake of fire.

THE FLOW OF JUDGEMENTS
1) This is important for understanding the sequence of events.
(Rev 4:-5 KJV) *{5}* And out of the throne proceeded lightnings and thunderings and voices: and *there were* seven lamps of fire burning before the throne, which are the seven Spirits of God.

After this appears scroll with seals.

2) (Rev 8:1-2 KJV) And when he had opened the seventh seal, there was silence in heaven about the space of half an hour. *{2}* And I saw the seven angels which stood before God; and to them were given seven trumpets.

3) (Rev 15:5-6 KJV) And after that I looked, and, behold, the temple of the tabernacle of the testimony in heaven was opened: *{6}* And the seven angels came out of the temple, having the seven plagues, clothed in pure and white linen, and having their breasts girded with golden girdles.

The vials come out of last trumpet.
To John is revealed three phases rather than three separate judgments. If these were separate, then certain questions would arise. **1)** The 6th seal shows the setting of the second coming .*(Math24v30-31)*,and the gathering of the elect. The 5th trumpet shows five-month assault on beast's kingdom and 6th trumpet shows a war destroying 1/3 of all humanity. How do you place trumpet events when Jesus tells us the tribulation is over at the time of the gathering? (before 7th seal) **2)**When the 7th trumpet sounds and the angel declares it is finished,(the mystery of God) is this when the 1st vial causes pestilence to fall on kingdom of the beast and later the kings of the east come? Of course not, they not only end in harmony, I believe they start in harmony.

116

THE FOCUS OF JUDGEMENTS

CREATION

(focus)		(attributes)	(judgment)
1ST	Earth	Place of fruitfulness	Vegetation destroyed
2nd	Sea	Place of wealth & Busn.	Sea life and ships destroyed.
3rd	Rivers	Waters of life	Waters of life Poisoned. justice for Slain prophets.
4th	Sun	Enduring glory& blessing.Psm72v17,84v11	The glory departs curse of heat.

MANKIND

5th	Man of sin	Place of authority	Pain and disease.
6th	Armies of earth	Warfare	Armies destroyed
7th	Un-repented man	Pride of nations	Fire

THE FINAL JUDGMENT / THE SEVENTH SEAL, TRUMPET & VIAL

There is nothing to compare with the horror of Gods final judgment upon an un-repented world.

THE PRELUDE

The Sixth Seal is but a prelude to what is about to come. Calamity strikes the earth right after the Sixth Seal is opened. Zech 14v4-5 implies that Jesus descending upon the Mount of Olives in the Day of the Lord produces a worldwide earthquake that literally moves mountains and Islands out of their place. Combined with a worldwide meteor shower, a shock wave will roll through the atmosphere and Armageddon will come to an abrupt halt, as all mankind flees for refuge. Seven thousand will die in Jerusalem alone *(multiply that by all the cities in the earth)* which the scriptures say will trigger the release of faithful followers of Christ.

(Rev 6:12-17 KJV) And I beheld when he had opened the sixth seal, and, lo, there was a great earthquake; and the sun became black as sackcloth of hair, and the moon became as blood; *{13}* And the stars of heaven fell unto the earth, even as a fig tree casteth her untimely figs, when she is shaken of a mighty wind. *{14}* And the heaven departed as a scroll when it is rolled together; and every mountain and island were moved out of their places. *{15}* And the kings of the earth, and the great men, and the rich men, and the chief captains, and the mighty men, and every bondman, and every free man, hid themselves in the dens and in the rocks of the mountains; *{16}* And said to the mountains and rocks, Fall on us, and hide us from the face of him that sitteth on the throne, and from the wrath of the Lamb: *{17}* For the great day of his wrath is come; and who shall be able to stand?

(Rev 11:12-15 KJV) And they heard a great voice from heaven saying unto them, Come up hither. And they ascended up to heaven in a cloud; and their enemies beheld them. *{13}* And the same hour was there a great earthquake, and the tenth part of the city fell, and in the earthquake were

118

slain of men seven thousand: and the remnant were affrighted, and gave glory to the God of heaven. *{14}* The second woe is past; *and,* behold, the third woe cometh quickly

THE SEVENTH JUDGMENT

Rev 11:15 And the seventh angel sounded; and there were great voices in heaven, saying, The kingdoms of this world are become the kingdoms of our Lord, and of his Christ; and he shall reign for ever and ever.:16 And the four and twenty elders, which sat before God on their seats, fell upon their faces, and worshipped God,:17 Saying, We give thee thanks, O Lord God Almighty, which art, and wast, and art to come; because thou hast taken to thee thy great power, and hast reigned.:18 And the nations were angry, and thy wrath is come, and the time of the dead, that they should be judged, and that thou shouldest give reward unto thy servants the prophets, and to the saints, and them that fear thy name, small and great; and shouldest destroy them which destroy the earth.
:19 And the temple of God was opened in heaven, and there was seen in his temple the ark of his testament: and there were lightnings, and voices, and thunderings, and an earthquake, and great hail.

The greatest earthquake the world has ever known or could imagine takes place. The proud have their request granted because here the mountains and islands are not moved, they are no more! Every mountain has been leveled and every island submerged. Hailstones rain upon the entire planet and millions are stoned to death. The earth has been knocked off her axis and wobbles through space like a drunk. The world is on fire. Peter tells us the elements are literally melting away. (Rev11v16-20, Rev16v20-21, 2 Pet3v10)

The mystery of the Voices, Thunders and Lighting.
Revelation ch11v15 shows us this happens after the conclusion of Seventh Judgment

Voices we see in ch11v15

119

(Rev 11:15 KJV) And the seventh angel sounded; and there were great voices in heaven, saying, The kingdoms of this world are become *the kingdoms* of our Lord, and of his Christ; and he shall reign for ever and ever.........The voice of the Saints.

Thunders we see in ch 10v3

(Job 37:5 KJV) God thundereth marvellously with his voice; great things doeth he, which we cannot comprehend. (Rev 10:3-4 KJV) And cried with a loud voice, as *when* a lion roareth: and when he had cried, seven thunders uttered their voices. {4} And when the seven thunders had uttered their voices, I was about to write: and I heard a voice from heaven saying unto me, Seal up those things which the seven thunders uttered, and write them not. ......The thunder is God.

Lightning we see in ch18v1

(Rev 18:1 KJV) And after these things I saw another angel come down from heaven, having great power; and the earth was lightened with his glory. (Rev21v11 & 23)
(Psa 77:18 KJV) The voice of thy thunder *was* in the heaven: the lightnings lightened the world: the earth trembled and shook...
...The light is Jesus

Every time judgment is concluded there is a reaction in heaven. That's exciting because the saints will be judged and this is mentioned again -- this time with no record of earthquakes and hail.
(Rev 4:2 KJV) And immediately I was in the spirit; and, behold, a throne was set in heaven, and *one* sat on the throne....(:5) And out of the throne proceeded lightnings and thunderings and voices: and *there were* seven lamps of fire burning before the throne, which are the seven Spirits of God.

19
DESTINIES

There are **three major covenants** concerning Israel and the church.

Abraham: Gen12v7,13v15-16,15v18,Acts13v26 ,Gen. 22v18 and Gal.3v16. Promised a nation and land for the Jews.
Promised that from his seed all nations would be blessed.
.Isa10v22, 19v25, 43v1, Ezk34v24.

David: Promise of a never ending throne through a messiah. Psm89v3-4, Jerm33v22, 25v26, 2 Sam 7v12-16.

New Covenant:.Jerm31v31-34, The issues of new heart, forgiveness of sin and the law written in our inward parts. (Holy Spirit Ezk11v19).Ezk37v26,Heb8v8-13,13v24.

God will fulfill all his promise concerning destinies. It's important to note, none of these covenants conflict with the destinies of the Church.

Jesus will judge the world in righteousness. Acts17v31, Psm75v2, Psm146v10, Isa24v23 and Rm 15v12.

The Apostles and Prophets will judge the Jewish nation. Lk22v29-30, Ex19v6.

The Gentile believers of the first resurrection will judge the Gentile world with Christ.1Corth.6v2, 2Tim2v12. Also Rev5v9-10

The 144,000 will become priests and servants of the most high.Isa.66:19-21

The sea of glass we see empty in Rev4v6 before tribulation begins, we find in Rev15v2 filled with the martyred saints of tribulation. They have been resurrected. (Rev7v9) This scene in Rev20v4 is recorded in heaven. The word of God declares they have a special place of service in the temple. Rev7v15,Rev22v3.

Those that survive the Great Tribulation receive a new world with peace, long life and a perfect reign. Rev21v4, Isa35v5-10 & 65v16-17.

20
WALK THROUGH
LAST WEEKS OF TIME

1. REASON FOR ORDER

2. BEGINNING OF SORROWS

3. THE BEAST, SOUTH AND NORTH

4. ISRAELS FIRST COVENANT

5. THE REDEEMED OF ISRAEL

6. THE BLESSING OF LIFE

7. THE BEAST SUFFERS A REVERSAL

8. REVIVAL

9. THE BEHEADING BEGINS

10. THE THRONE ROOM

11. THE SEVEN SPIRITS OF GOD (1ST JUDGMENT)

12. 2ND- 4TH JUDGMENTS

13. VICTORY OF THE BEAST (5TH JUDGMENT)

14. THE DAY OF THE LORD (6TH JUDGMENT)

15. FINAL JUDGMENT

ORDER OF LAST DAYS

EVENTS	REASONING
1. Beginning of sorrows	(see walk through last weeks)

2.Seven year agreement.   Dan9v27 final wk.

3.Rapture of the church   Judgment of saints shown before that of earth. 2Thes.2v1-4 crowns received before judgment earth begins.2Tim4v8,Rev4v4 We see after Satan overcome by saints abomination begins. Rev12v10 -13,v17,Rev13v6-7. Thrones are set (Apostle & Prophets) before Judgement.Dan7v8-9,Rev4v2-4

4.Abomination that makes desolate   Bible show beast persecutes Jews and believers after defiling sanctuary.Dan11v31-35,Rev13v5-7, Rev12v13-17.Jesus says a Great Tribulation would begin with defiling of the sanctuary which is middle of final Week. Math24v15-21,Dan9v27,Rev13v5-6

5.Great tribulation   Jesus says begins with defiling of sanctuary. The defiling of the sanctuary is the revealing of the beast.2Thes2v3-4 One of marks of beast revealing is mouth of "blasphemy and great things"Rev13v5,Dan7v8, The seal trumpet & vial released after thrones set Rev5v1-7. Thrones are set after revealing of the beast. Compare Dan7v8-10 and Rev4v2-4, 5v9-12. The great tribulation is the persecution of the Jewish nation and out pouring of Gods indignation.

6.Armaggedon   World war in which God gathers the nations for judgment. Rev 16v14-16, Zeph3v8,Joel3v11-12, Signs are sun and moon darkened Isa.13v10, Joel2v31,before the Day of the Lord., Joel.3v12-14, Jer46v10, Rev11v18.

7.Day of the lord (Return of Christ) Begin's when Jesus stands on Mt. Olives producing and earthquake during the battle of Armageddon. Zech.14v4, Rev16v18-19, Rev11v13, Rev 6v12-13 Joel.3v15-16, Destroys armies of the world with hailstones and ends tribulation. Rev16v21, Rev.6v13-16....

Job38v22-23 Rev.11v19, Psm.18v7-15, Ends **Time of trouble** Isa.33v2-3,Jerm.30v7-8

8.Resurrection of Trib. Martyrs   Takes place after the judgment on the world's armies. Math.24v29-30, Dan.12v1-2, Zech.14v4-5, Psm18v13-16.

9.Beast Thrown in the lake of fire, devil locked away, un-repented destroyed Rev19v20-21, ch20v1-2, Rev14v14-20, Dan7v11,Isa.14v19-20

10 Christ receives the kingdom 1000yr reign   Dan.7v11-14, 25-27, Rev 20:4-7

11. Devil loosed and deceives. After 1000yrs. Devil judged with Gog and Magog, Great white throne judgement.Rev.20v12

12. New Heaven ,New Earth Rev 21:1-4, Isa.65v17.

Walk Through The Last Weeks of Time

I believe chpt.24 of Mathew covers the events we see in Rev ch4 thru 20. In this section we take a detailed walk tying in other relating prophecy. There are many other characters and events not covered in previous materials placed here in their relation to the larger picture.

The Beginning of Sorrows.
Matt 24:4-8 I Tim 4:1-5 & II Tim 3:1-9.

Intro: I place the beginning of sorrows before the seven-year agreement with the Beast. These are worldwide conditions that seem to intensify, birth pains. They are not uncommon to man. What's unique is that they'll exist simultaneously and will intensify with time. Jesus speaks of a Great Tribulation unlike any the world has ever experienced. The 1st judgment being one third of earths vegetation destroyed and the food source of possibly 3 billion people destroyed, this is more than sorrow. Theres no indicators for when the beginning of sorrows begin. Before the seven year agreement we see warfare involving no less than five nations with the Beastly empire through at least seven reigns. These conflicts we know span more than four years before Daniel's middle of the week. Dan 11:8 &13-14 & Dan 11:18-21 & 11:28. Daniel doesn't speak of the sorrows added by Jesus. To assume Christ was including them into a frame of 7 years would be to also put the parable of fig tree in the same frame. Even as I write, the last two decades have been plagued with consistent wars, famine, and earthquakes.

The bible also speaks of social deterioration. Self-interest, self-gratification and self-indulgence will rule. Deceptions of all sorts will increase. Many deceivers will arise. Gurus such as Rajneesh, Muktananda and Sai baba have been claimed by followers to be the divine one. I believe Jesus is giving us the signs of a closing era whose last events are yet to come. These will truly be perilous times.

THE WALK BEGINS!
Another intellectual bows to one who is all knowing. The answer to peace and power and destiny are found in self. A new generation has arisen whose daily diet is witchcraft, sorcery & deception. Corruption has become a way of life. Self and pleasure are gods. Sex outside of marriage, adultery, homosexuality, abortion and bestiality have become the norm and not the exception. Those who label these practices unethical unclean or sin are viewed as narrow minded and dangerous to the community -- the world community. Those who deal in the occult, in need of a fix, are only a speed dial away with a small fee per minute. Your palm can be read along with horoscope in privacy of your own residence, courtesy of the Internet. In the media the plight of famine is as common as the latest natural disaster. Seasonal weather has become unpredictable. A new disease has surfaced with no known cure destroying thousands.

This added to the already several viruses that also without cure are leading multi-millions to their death.

There is also a great falling away from fundamental Christianity. Around the world many churches have become museums, meeting halls and social service centers. Yet heart failure is on the increase because of fear, and there is war and several unsolved conflicts around the world. Culture against culture, tribe against tribe and race against race. They fight for land, compensation, religion, power and pride. Rumor has it a greater conflict is in the making for Israel. Jesus said be not troubled, the end is not yet.

The Beast, Dan 11:7-32, Dan 7:24-25,Rev ch13, ch 17 & ch 12. A kingdom emerges, a union of nations once known as the Roman Empire; Dan's forth beast. They are now undoubtedly a major force in the earth even with internal struggles and friction between member nations. They're a world superpower. Chapter 11 of Daniel begins with Alexander the Great of Greece (Daniel 8:21) and his 4 horns. Verse 4 tells us Alexander conquest was divided by four of his generals. *(The four winds of heaven chapter 11:4 & chapter 8:8).* Yet we are pointed to the horn of the south. Chapter 11:5. The greatest of 4 generals located south was Seleocus of Babylonia. He became the Greatest and ruled all of Syria and Asia Minor. (Encarta 97) Dan 11:7 talks about a branch of her roots. This break in time brings us to the days just before final week of Daniel (compare Isaiah 11v1-2)

The mystery is the daughter produced a branch that is now part of the revised Roman Empire, (*this could possibly be Lydia which was part of ancient Asia minor and believed by Greek historians to be homeland of the Etruscan people, early Italians.*) The south was taken over by the Arabs and today represents nations or a nation in the Middle East.

God starts us with the 6th ruler whose Arms are responsible for the South's defeat. He prevails and becomes unstoppable. No information is given about the five previous leaders. This is exactly what the Lord reveals in Rev 17:10

And there are seven kings: five are fallen, and one is, *and* the other is not yet come; and when he cometh, he must continue a short space. (Rev 17:11 KJV) And the beast that was, and is not, even he is the eighth, and is of the seven, and goeth into perdition.

(Dan 11:19-21 KJV) Then he shall turn his face toward the fort of his own land: but he shall stumble and fall, and not be found. {20} Then shall stand up in his estate a raiser of taxes *in* the glory of the kingdom: but within few days he shall be destroyed, neither in anger, nor in battle. {21} And in his estate shall stand up a vile person, to whom they shall not give the honour of the kingdom: but he shall come in peaceably, and obtain the kingdom by flatteries.

Why does God in Rev17 and Dan11 begin with the sixth ruler? This could be because this is the **first covenant** made with Israel. The covenant with antichrist is the following covenant. God wants us to know what covenant to watch for. Perceiving wrong signs and not seeing expected results could be the reason the love of many grew cold. Dan11v16 reveals after the victory over the south he stands in the glorious land with destruction in his power. In verse 17 the word upright ones Yashar: means straight convent equity just. Israel is forced into and agreement with the "daughter of women."*(the term "daughter of" is commonly used in old test. for a nation and people Psm45v12, Isa10v30 , Ezk23v2-4)* She shall be beneficial in Israel's survival, though not the original intent.

The Beast is off to battle again with his face toward the coastlands but a problem arising in his own empire draws him home. This brings his downfall. His successor shall stand up

128

and raise taxes on Israel, but Rev 17 & Dan 11 says his term is short.

The Antichrist as in most novels of the past, he's the vile one. He's been in power before. Yet it is mentioned he shall not receive the honor of the kingdom. Yet he is peaceable, patient and wins them by (diplomacy) flatteries. Once established, he destroys his opposition including the prince of the covenant. This is the initiator, author or establisher of the covenant made with the Sixth Beast. Now Israel makes a covenant with the "vile one". This is the awaited sign. After this point it's called **The Holy Covenant**.

((Exo 31:16-17 KJV) Wherefore the children of Israel shall keep the sabbath, to observe the sabbath throughout their generations, *for* a perpetual covenant. *{17}* It *is* a sign between me and the children of Israel for ever: for *in* six days the LORD made heaven and earth, and on the seventh day he rested, and was refreshed.

(Jer 34:13-14 KJV) Thus saith the LORD, the God of Israel; I made a covenant with your fathers in the day that I brought them forth out of the land of Egypt, out of the house of bondmen, saying, *{14}* At the end of seven years let ye go every man his brother an Hebrew, which hath been sold unto thee; and when he hath served thee six years, thou shalt let him go free from thee: but your fathers hearkened not unto me, neither inclined their ear.

Some where in this time period the temple has been restored for Hebrew worship & daily sacrifices instituted. The covenant is for seven years, it also includes an Arms agreement.

The Redeemed of Israel...

.(Hosea 3:3 KJV) And I said unto her, Thou shalt abide for me many days; thou shalt not play the harlot, and thou shalt not be for *another* man: so *will* I also *be* for thee.

For the children of Israel shall abide many days without a king, and without a prince, and without a sacrifice, and without an image, and without an ephod, and *without* teraphim: Afterward shall the children of Israel return, and seek the LORD their God, and David their king; and shall fear the LORD and his goodness in the latter days.

Right before this agreement the daughter of Zion flees into the wilderness. *(144,000)* Paul says in Rom 11:25- For I would not, brethren, that ye should be ignorant of this mystery, lest ye should be wise in your own conceits; that blindness in part is happened to Israel, until the fulness of the Gentiles be come in.

The wilderness is symbolic of testing, preparation and dependency for Gods people and his prophets. (Luke 1:76-80) For three and a half years the remnant is in the wilderness. During this time Jeremiah the prophet gives a prophecy of what the vile one will be doing in this time period.

The Lord said, Verily it shall be well with thy remnant; verily I will cause the enemy to entreat thee *well* in the time of evil and in the time of affliction. Shall iron break the northern iron and the steel? Thy substance and thy treasures will I give to the spoil with out price, and that for all thy sins, even in all thy boarders.((Jer 15:11-13 KJV)

The time clock for Daniel's seventieth week is about to begin. This agreement between the Jews and the vile one marks the final seven years of our time. Dan9v27.

THE BLESSING OF LIFE

Though warfare and calamity are a common occurrence. I believe this will be a time of great prosperity for developing nations. Childbirths will have greatly decreased so families will be smaller. There will be a constant demand to fill positions created by deaths due to disease, catastrophes and crime.

The pleasure industries shall boom. The bible reveals as well as history that judgment often came upon nations at the height of their prosperity. Gen13v10,Ex12v35-36,Nahm2v8-13,Rev3v15-17. Christians shall also prosper and there shall be a great falling away. Many who profess Christ shall be drawn into lifestyles of comfort and ease. Compromise will come easy and complacency common.... *A dreadful sound is in his ears: in prosperity the destroyer shall come upon him. Job 15:21* (also..Lk17v28, Mth24v37-39, 2Thes.2v1-3)

Sorrows continue. Earthquakes, war, famine and corruption. The vile one begins to violate the league, builds up arms and moves into the riches places of the province. He does something former leaders have not done in the conquest of nations. He dispenses the riches and the spoils. This kingdom of the beast had been a kingdom that had not conquered other nations for spoil or material gain. Yet the vile one does. Israel is not defenseless because he must plan to take her strong holds. Again he's off to war for another conquest to the South.

Major War- arrayed in battle, two Great Armies the kingdom of the Beast *(Rome Revised)* and king of the South *(Arab Coalition)* and their allies. There is a conspiracy. The King of the south is betrayed by two of his allies. *(This is possibly Dan11 verse 43 Lybians & Ethopians)*. With this victory the vile one is greatly exalted, and greatly enriched by spoils of the south. His heart is set against the holy covenant as he returns to his land.

Then appears Two Witness. The Bible tells us they have a 3 1\2 year ministry and are resurrected during the 6th judgment. This places them before the breaking of the holy covenant and the place of their ministry Jerusalem. (Rev 11 & Zech 11:2-3) They begin to proclaim the word of God. Not just to Israel but to the world.

At the time of their ministry it is suggested in Rev 11:6, there will be no rain. Drought will begin on the face of the earth. This is the beginning of their ministry. We have no idea when they come nor how. Will they as our Lord and John the Baptist grow from youth or be translated Old Testament prophets. "Jesus did say Elijah shall come."

The **Beast** **suffers a reversal**. He had planned and executed another assault on the south but the great unexpected happens. Who would ever believe the ships of Cypress could deal him a defeat. He returns to his land and his hatred for the holy covenant grows. At the same time of this earthly event, there's one in Heaven -- another reversal for the dragon. **The church has overcome** by the word of their testimony and the blood of the lamb. They've been resurrected. (Dan.11v29-31 & Rev.12v9-17) Jesus records this...

(Mat 24:40 KJV) Then shall two be in the field; the one shall be taken, and the other left.(Mat 24:41 KJV) Two *women shall be* grinding at the mill; the one shall be taken, and the other left.

There will be no one in the field and nothing to mill when Jesus returns. Men will be hidden in caves in great fear in that hour. There's no longer a place in heaven for the accuser, he's cast down. The bible say's "rejoice oh heaven!" Paul comments on this event.

(2 Th 2:7) For the mystery of iniquity doth already work: only he who now letteth *will let,* until he be taken out of the way.:8 And then shall that Wicked be revealed, whom the Lord shall consume with the spirit of his mouth, and shall destroy with the brightness of his coming:

The beast is grieved because of his defeat. He begins his conspiracy to break the holy covenant with others who forsake the covenant. Now is the time to implement his mark on the peoples of the world, and his image. At this point the world is at his feet. (Rev 13:4 KJV)

The false prophet has convinced the world, through great signs, even fire from heaven (a world that already worships the dragon) to make him an image. Yes the world makes the **Image of the Beast**.(*Conjecture: it is highly possibly that worship of the beast is an act of voluntarily accepting the mark or the name or the number of his name. I say this because he's "Granted Power" to persecute the believers after the abomination. How are the believers identified?*) Rev 13. What better time is there to assault the last group of intolerance to world unity? Israel the Zionist burden of the nations.

Revival, the remnant returns from the wilderness. These are Hebrews that know their God. *(Dan 11:32)* They begin to utter their revelation like John the Baptist. The two prophets give testimony and the children's hearts return to the father. Recently believers around the globe have disappeared and some who knew them now believe.

Forces March, the morning report around the globe broadcasts.. **...The beast and her allies seize Jerusalem**. There seems to be no resistance and its made clear in Dan11v32 many officials are won by flattery. Yet the whole story is to be told. The bible says "They" in Dan 11:31 which could imply beast and false prophets or ten kings with no kingdom. It could also imply a police force (*possibly including traitorous Jews. Zeph3v4*). Their forces spoil Jerusalem. They stop the daily sacrifice and pollute the sanctuary. Now the warning of Jesus is clear

(Mat 24:15-18 KJV) When ye therefore shall see the abomination of desolation, spoken of by Daniel the prophet, stand in the holy place, (whoso readeth, let him understand:) Then let them which be in Judaea flee into the mountains:

133

Let him which is on the housetop not come down to take any thing out of his house: let him which is in the field return not back to take his clothes.

A TIME TO HIDE…The picture is clear around the world. Backsliders and others left behind are faced with the terror they've tried to deny. The man of sin has been revealed! Many that day will not log in, sign in nor come in, just slowly slip away. Others will desire to escape, but to where is their fear. No longer is there a place in the middle. Identify with the beast or die!

THE BEHEADING BEGINS (see the elect or trib. martyrs): They begin to persecute the redeemed of God but they do exploits and escape their hands. Though world forces pursue the 144,000 witnesses are graced by Gods intervention. For many days it continues -- those that understand instruct many but their end is martyrdom. The beast has set up the Image, verse 31 of Dan 11 says something is "place" in sanctuary fortress. The Image is activated by the false prophet. It speaks and has the power to hand out death sentences to non-worshipers.
 (Rev 13:15) Around the globe worship is now mandatory. The method in judging non-worshipers the bible reveals is beheading.

The 1st Judgment. (Read Rev 4:5&6) The scene turns to heaven. John is told to come up so he could receive revelation of what would happen after this. (Rev 4:1) After what? THE CHURCH ERA. The first three chapters of the book Revelation. This is called the time of the Gentiles. The break between Dan 69th & 70th week. Luke 21:24 & Dan9v26-27 .(see breaks in time) John had a message for the churches surrounding Patmos but he also had a prophetic message for the generations to come. John was lifted for revelation beyond the churches.

He saw the sea of glass and the redeemed nations of tribulations Rev 15:2-4. He saw the four beasts, the four faces and revelations of Christ, the lion of royalty (Book of Matt), the calf or servanthood (Book of Mark), the man or humanity of (book of Luke) and the eagle, the divinity of Christ (Book of John). See Also Ezk, 1:10.

At this point we understand that after the church's departure the following events in heaven lead to conclusion of prophecy. In chapter 5 the book with Seven Seals is revealed and the occasion is the judgment on mankind. John saw twenty-four thrones with elders, clothed in white robes, the righteousness of the saints, (Isa 61::10 & Rev. 3:4-5) and golden crowns. God's reward for the saints is a crown. In (2 Tim.4:8), the Greek word Stephanos means victor's crown! The judgment seat of Christ is over. The fire has tried their works, they've received their rewards and the thrones are set.

The Day of Christ is about to begin……..Wherefore, *as* I live, saith the Lord GOD; Surely, because thou hast defiled my sanctuary with all thy detestable things, and with all thine abominations, therefore will I also diminish *thee;* neither shall mine eye spare, neither will I have any pity. *{12}* A third part of thee shall die with the pestilence, and with famine shall they be consumed in the midst of thee: and a third part shall fall by the sword round about thee; and I will scatter a third part into all the winds, and I will draw out a sword after them. (Ezek 5:11-12 KJV)

THE THRONE ROOM (Rev.4-6)
The setting is wonderful,….. it was foretold by Daniel.

(Dan 7:9 KJV) I beheld till the thrones were cast down, and the Ancient of days did sit, whose garment was white as snow, and the hair of his head like the pure wool: his throne was like the fiery flame, and his wheels as burning fire.(:10) A fiery stream issued and came forth from before him: thousand thousands ministered unto him, and ten thousand times ten thousand stood before him: the judgment was set, and the books were opened.

The Ancient of days sat on the throne --Jesus Christ. Before Him are the thrones promised and given to Apostles & Prophets.

. (Mat 19:27 KJV) Then answered Peter and said unto him, Behold, we have forsaken all, and followed thee; what shall we have therefore? (Mat 19:28 KJV) And Jesus said unto them, Verily I say unto you, That ye which have followed me, in the regeneration when the Son of man shall sit in the throne of his glory, ye also shall sit upon twelve thrones, judging the twelve tribes of Israel.

Here we see them on the thrones. The regeneration means to make all things new. Here again is the wonderful accuracy of scripture. Look at the order of Dan chpt.7. In verse 8 pompous little horn (revealed), verse 9 the thrones in place, verse 10 court seated, books opened and verse 11 pompous horn judged in burning flame. In verse 13-14 we see the Son of man with a cloud (which symbolizes the Second Coming) who receives the kingdom from the Father. It's important to note after the court was seated **the books** are opened. Don't let the phrase "books open" throw you. There are more than one set of books mentioned in the book of Revelation. One has seals and is opened at removal of the judgment.

Zec 5:1-3 KJV) Then I turned, and lifted up mine eyes, and looked, and behold a flying roll. {2} And he said unto me, What seest thou? And I answered, I see a flying roll; the length thereof *is* twenty cubits, and the breadth thereof ten cubits. {3} Then said he unto me, This *is* the curse that goeth forth over the face of the whole earth: for every one that stealeth shall be cut off *as* on this side according to it; and every one that sweareth shall be cut off *as* on that side according to it

One is little book that John the apostle ate like Ezekiel. (Rev. 10:8-11)

The other set we have in Rev20v12, the book of life and the book of records. (Mat 12:36-37 KJV)
The horn has eyes like a man and a mouth. The devil always needs a mouthpiece and this one called the beast is burned at the final judgment and the dragon locked away. Rev 19:19-21
.

(Rev 4:5 KJV) And out of the throne proceeded lightnings and thunderings and voices: and *there were* seven lamps of fire burning before the throne, which **are the seven Spirits of God.**

These are Spirits of God unlike the four spirits of heaven. *(four horses of Zech1v12-13)* These are symbolized as lamps, horns and eyes and represent the eyes of the lord. The flame is the divine presence of God, the horn dignity and strength.

(Dan 10:6 KJV) His body also *was* like the beryl, and his face as the appearance of lightning, and his eyes as **lamps of fire**, and his arms and his feet like in colour to polished brass, and the voice of his words like the voice of a multitude.
Zech. Speaking of seven lamps..(Zec 4:10 KJV) For who hath despised the day of small things? for they shall rejoice, and shall see the plummet in the hand of Zerubbabel *with* those seven; they *are* the eyes of the LORD, which run to and fro through the whole earth.
(2 Chr 16:9 KJV) For the eyes of the LORD run to and fro throughout the whole earth, to show himself strong in the behalf of *them* whose heart *is* perfect toward him. Herein thou hast done foolishly: therefore from henceforth thou shalt have wars.also Rev 4:5,5v6,Zec4v10,Rev3v1

What a beautiful picture we have before judgments begins. The Lamb of God is looking to deliver those who hearts are toward him. You will find all these scriptures deal with end time prophecy. The Lion of the tribe of Judah is worthy, the saints of heaven rejoice (Rev 5:9-14) and the **Lamb of God opens the 1st Seal.**

The White horse rider goes forth to conquer. . (Hab 3:5) Before him went the pestilence, and burning coals went forth at his feet. One third of the world's trees and green grass is destroyed. The will of God is the conquering of the nations. Pestilence falls upon those with the mark of the beast. The world is in wonder and the prophets make it clear, the judgment of God has come. The 144,000 are now permeating the nations with the gospel message and the warning -- don't take the mark!

(Isa 66:19 KJV) And I will set a sign among them, and I will send those that escape of them unto the nations, *to* Tarshish, Pul, and Lud, that draw the bow, *to* Tubal, and Javan, *to* the isles afar off, that have not heard my fame, neither have seen my glory; and they shall declare my glory among the Gentiles.

The self-made god, the Beast begins to regroup. He starts by denouncing all other god's, he has the wisdom to bring harmony. Yet the two witnesses continue their ministry. *(It is possible that the witness prophesied first five judgments)* Rev11:4-10. The bible tells us the beast popularity grows.

(Isa 32:18 KJV) And my people shall dwell in a peaceable habitation, and in sure dwellings, and in quiet resting places;(:19) When it shall hail, coming down on the forest; and the city shall be low in a low place.

The 2nd Judgment

The 2nd Judgment

The seal is broken and the will of God is the Red Horse, "War" and he was to take peace from the earth. The Trumpet sounds. A great mountain with fire is cast into the sea, not from heaven but cast. One third of ships in the sea destroyed with sea life, the Vial pours and its completion means no peace. The sea becomes as the blood of dead men. Rev 16:3. (This is possibly Dan 11v40-43 which symbolizes major worldwide conflict.)

The war continues, yet this is more than the curse of war. The word peace means harmony, things working together, their will be no harmony in this day. In individual lives and in nations the void of emptiness, despair and frustration will grow like a great canyon.

The 3rd judgment

The black horse with balances: balances are what we call scales today, tool for determining valve. This interpreted is a bag of grocery for a day's wages.

(Amos 5:7) Ye who turn judgment to wormwood, and leave off righteousness in the earth,

Famine begins. Prices rise, God in heaven declared it. The Seals broken the trumpet blows and great star from heaven falls on 1\3 of earth's fresh water supply. The water is poisoned. No rain and economic madness. Wormwood is a symbol of bitter calamity. *Lam 3:15, Jerm 9:15 & 23:15.* Black market vendors sell bottles of water for gold jewelry or what ever inflated value they can. The entire world has gone to food rationing. Many third world nations whose power depends on hydroelectric power plants will almost shut down. 1\3 of the world vegetation is destroyed with no hope of recovery for lack of rain. Farmers depending on irrigation now watch crops wither away. Those that can are now under the control of local Governments and watch their life's sweat shipped off to the war effort. Yes the war, when will it stop? The beast has entered the glorious land again, and wormwood continues to spread, not in just one region. This black horse moves to in fro in the earth until all the waters are blood Zech 1:8-10 (Amos 5:7 KJV)

4th Judgment

The beast with the face of an eagle says to John come and see. (Rev 4;7 & 6:1-8) A pale *(Greenish)* horse, death sat upon him and hell followed him. Death a creation for the judgment of sin, along with hell also called the finally enemy, with war and famine. Many begin to perish by firearms, force and aggression. The Sword: symbol of the earliest weapon. Lack of water and food are causing the deaths of millions, and there is the light. Hab.3:11-12. One third of stars, sun and moon with hold their light. *Possibly the smoke of great warfare against the Arab alliances.*

Problems in the Heavens.
There's a phenomenon of fierce heat and the blocking of the sun. The elderly die by thousands from the heat, locked in homes that they fear to exit. What has happen to the ozone? This is beyond sunburn. People are now greatly limited in their movement. The remaining outdoor vegetation dries out as the landscape begins to look like a desert. Rivers and streams are running dry. Desperate animals of prey turn to man's dwelling place for shelter and food. Rogue animals are everywhere. A generation of drug addicts is in a frantic frenzy and darkness is the only time any one dares to venture out. (Rev 7:16 & 16:9, Dan 11:40-43) The Jewish Evangelists are seeing many converted, unstopped and undetected by the world's system. The call comes from the desert. Christ is here, He has returned, as they seek to lure many from hiding who have not worshiped the Beast.

Victory of the Beast
The beast has gone out against his enemies and he is the victor. He and his coalition defeat the Kings of the South and many other nations. Only Edom, Moab & Ammon escape. He has

gained many resources and the Ethiopians and Libyans are in his alliance. He continues to prosper as the false prophet plays his song, "who is like the beast," he knows what it is to suffer and knows what it is to start again. He was mortally wounded. He has survived and he will lead us to recovery. *(Note: Rev13 says one of the seven heads of the Beast was mortally wounded and the wound was healed. Rev chpt17 tells us this is one of the first seven leaders of the empire of the beast and could very well be the beast Himself)*

(1 Th 5:3 KJV) For when they shall say, Peace and safety; then sudden destruction cometh upon them, as travail upon a woman with child; and they shall not escape.

The 5th Judgment

Declarations are made by an angel, "woe, woe, woe!" Woe is a word denoting grief. The next three judgments are judgments of great grief. The atmosphere in heaven has changed, the seal is broken but John is not called to see. Yet from the altar John sees the **souls of those slain for the testimony of the word of God** from Able to Zechariah, Zechariah being slain between the temple & altar . These souls cry out "how long", holy and true before you give us justice of the hard hearted of this earth. (Matt 23:35-36) They're told to wait until those whom even at that moment were being slain for their faith in Jesus Christ because of their refusal to worship the beast or receive his mark. (Rev 6:10-11 & 20:4.)
They were slaughtered by numbers too numerous to name. (Rev 7:9) When their time is fulfilled justice will come. We see a beautiful picture of the martyred saints after the tribulation in Rev chapter 7. In their hands palms, symbols of victory and white robes symbols of righteousness. This victory came at a great price

(Rev 20:4 KJV) ......: and *I saw* the souls of them that were beheaded for the witness of Jesus, and for the word of God, and which had not worshipped the beast, neither his image, neither had received *his* mark upon their foreheads, or in their hands; and they lived and reigned with Christ a thousand years.

There is a special place in the heart of our Lord for his martyrs.
(Rev 14:13 KJV) And I heard a voice from heaven saying unto me, Write, Blessed *are* the dead which die in the Lord from henceforth: Yea, saith the Spirit, that they may rest from their labours; and their works do follow them.

Saints under the altar receive their white robes and with the rest of the heavenly host await the next event, the trumpet sounds.

(Rev 9:1-11 KJV) And the fifth angel sounded, and I saw a star fall from heaven unto the earth: and to him was given the key of the bottomless pit. {2} And he opened the bottomless pit; and there arose a smoke out of the pit, as the smoke of a great furnace; and the sun and the air were darkened by reason of the smoke of the pit. {3} And there came out of the smoke locusts upon the earth: and unto them was given power, as the scorpions of the earth have power.
{4} And it was commanded them that they should not hurt the grass of the earth, neither any green thing, neither any tree; but only those men which have not the seal of God in their foreheads. {5} And to them it was given that they should not kill them, but that they should be tormented five months: and their torment *was* as the torment of a scorpion, when he striketh a man. {6} And in those days shall men seek death, and shall not find it; and shall desire to die, and death shall flee from them. {7} And the shapes of the locusts *were* like unto horses prepared unto battle; and on their heads *were* as it were crowns like gold, and their faces *were* as the faces of men. {8} And they had hair as the hair of women, and their teeth were as *the teeth* of lions. {9} And they had breastplates, as it were breastplates of iron; and the sound of their wings *was* as the sound of chariots of many horses running to battle. {10} And they had tails like unto scorpions, and there were stings in their tails: and their power *was* to hurt men five months. {11} And they had a king over them, *which is* the

angel of the bottomless pit, whose name in the Hebrew tongue *is* Abaddon, but in the Greek tongue hath *his* name Apollyon

The Vial is poured.

(Rev 16:10-11 KJV) And the fifth angel poured out his vial upon the seat of the beast; and his kingdom was full of darkness; and they gnawed their tongues for pain, *{11}* And blasphemed the God of heaven because of their pains and their sores, and repented not of their deeds.

(Nahum 3:17 KJV) Thy crowned *are* as the locusts, and thy captains as the great grasshoppers, which camp in the hedges in the cold day, *but* when the sun ariseth they flee away, and their place is not known where they *are.*

The darkness lifts and the messenger comes. The beast is troubled. A two hundred million-man army is coming against him.

The Sixth Judgment

The Sixth Seal is broken and there is a great earthquake. The sun was blackened and the moon became blood. This is the will of God. The earthquake is the marker and the sun darkened with a blood moon. Jesus made this clear so there would be no doubt. This is the prophecy long awaited by prophets of old and apostles of new.

The Day of the Lord. Joel3:15-16, Zech 14:3-5, God's will is created, Armageddon begins. In Rev 9:14-15 the trumpet sounds. On earth the beast sees clearly his enemies' objective is Palestine (*Speculation. Possibly the only place on earth with greenery and with resources*).
Troop movement from east and north. Battles erupting! There is no restraint on the weapons being used. They are destroying the

earth! He rises up in a great fury of retaliation. The casualties on both sides come to one third of all mankind.

The sixth angel pores his vial. (Rev 16:12-16 KJV) And the sixth angel poured out his vial upon the great river Euphrates; and the water thereof was dried up, that the way of the kings of the east might be prepared. *{13}* And I saw three unclean spirits like frogs *come* out of the mouth of the dragon, and out of the mouth of the beast, and out of the mouth of the false prophet. *{14}* For they are the spirits of devils, working miracles, *which* go forth unto the kings of the earth and of the whole world, to gather them to the battle of that great day of God Almighty. *{15}* Behold, I come as a thief. Blessed *is* he that watcheth, and keepeth his garments, lest he walk naked, and they see his shame. *{16}* And he gathered them together into a place called in the Hebrew tongue Armageddon.
(Dan 11:45 KJV) And he shall plant the tabernacles of his palace between the seas in the glorious holy mountain; yet he shall come to his end, and none shall help him.

The Final Stand… The Beast, kings of the east and their coalition are taking advantage of the Euphrates drying. Egypt and her allies have gathered themselves again for the last conflict. The entire world is closing in on Jerusalem.
(Dan 11:45) And he (the beast) shall plant the tabernacles of his palace between the seas in the glorious holy mountain; ……

(Joel 2:30-31 KJV) And I will show wonders in the heavens and in the earth, blood, and fire, and pillars of smoke. *{31}* The sun shall be turned into darkness, and the moon into blood, before the great and the terrible day of the LORD come.

The battle rages-the two witnesses cry out, this truly is the last hour. Yet like Pharaoh of old, the heart of the world is stone. Their testimony is done, they are finally assaulted and over come and the world rejoices. Rev 11:8-10.We shouldn't be amazed in a world today that applauds the adulator and winks at the wicked prevailing in wickedness. The witness's bodies are laid out for public display.

(From this point on I will use scriptures pertaining to the Day of the Lord placed in prophetic order.)

(Amos 5:18-20 KJV) Woe unto you that desire the day of the LORD! to what end *is* it for you? the day of the LORD *is* darkness, and not light. *{19}* As if a man did flee from a lion, and a bear met him; or went into the house, and leaned his hand on the wall, and a serpent bit him. *{20}* *Shall* not the day of the LORD *be* darkness, and not light? even very dark, and no brightness in it?

(Ezk 30:3-9 KJV) For the day *is* near, even the day of the LORD *is* near, a cloudy day; it shall be the time of the heathen. *{4}* And the sword shall come upon Egypt, and great pain shall be in Ethiopia, when the slain shall fall in Egypt, and they shall take away her multitude, and her foundations shall be broken down. *{5}* Ethiopia, and Libya, and Lydia, and all the mingled people, and Chub, and the men of the land that is in league, shall fall with them by the sword. *{6}* Thus saith the LORD;

They also that uphold Egypt shall fall; and the pride of her power shall come down: from the tower of Syene shall they fall in it by the sword, saith the Lord GOD. *{7}* And they shall be desolate in the midst of the countries *that are* desolate, and her cities shall be in the midst of the cities *that are* wasted. *{8}* And they shall know that I *am* the LORD, when I have set a fire in Egypt, and *when* all her helpers shall be destroyed. *{9}* In that day shall messengers go forth from me in ships to make the careless Ethiopians afraid, and great pain shall come upon them, as in the day of Egypt: for, lo, it cometh.

(Joel 3:14 KJV) Multitudes, multitudes in the valley of decision: for the day of the LORD *is* near in the valley of decision.

(Zec 14:2 KJV) For I will gather all nations against Jerusalem to battle; and the city shall be taken, and the houses rifled, and the women ravished; and half of the city shall go forth into captivity, and the residue of the people shall not be cut off from the city.

Rev 16:15 KJV) Behold, I come as a thief. Blessed *is* he that watcheth, and keepeth his garments, lest he walk naked, and they see his shame.

(Job 38:22) Hast thou entered into the treasures of the snow? or hast thou seen the treasures of the hail, (:23) Which I have reserved against the time of trouble, against the day of battle and war?

(Rev 11:11-12 KJV) And after three days and an half the Spirit of life from God entered into them (the witnesses), and they stood upon their feet; and great fear fell upon them which saw them. *{12}* And they heard a great voice from heaven saying unto them, Come up hither. And they ascended up to heaven in a cloud; and their enemies beheld them.

(Rev 11:13 KJV) And the same hour was there a great earthquake, and the tenth part of the city fell, and in the earthquake were slain of men seven thousand: and the remnant were affrighted, and gave glory to the God of heaven.

(Rev 6:13 KJV) And the stars of heaven fell unto the earth, even as a fig tree casteth her untimely figs, when she is shaken of a mighty wind.

(Joel 3:16 KJV) The LORD also shall roar out of Zion, and utter his voice from Jerusalem; and the heavens and the earth shall shake: but the LORD *will be* the hope of his people, and the strength of the children of Israel.

(Zec 14:3 KJV) Then shall the LORD go forth, and fight against those nations, as when he fought in the day of battle. (Zep 1:10 KJV) And it shall come to pass in that day, saith the LORD, *that there shall be* the noise of a cry from the fish gate, and an howling from the second, and a great crashing from the hills.

(Zec 14:4-5 KJV) And his feet shall stand in that day upon the mount of Olives, which *is* before Jerusalem on the east, and the mount of Olives shall cleave in the midst thereof toward the east and toward the west, *and there shall be* a very great valley; and half of the mountain shall remove toward the north, and half of it toward the south. *{5}* And ye shall flee *to* the valley of the mountains; for the valley of the mountains shall reach unto Azal: yea, ye shall flee, like as ye fled from before the earthquake in the days of Uzziah king of Judah: and the LORD my God shall come, *and* all the saints with thee.

(Jer 46:10 KJV) For this *is* the day of the Lord GOD of hosts, a day of vengeance, that he may avenge him of his adversaries: and the sword shall devour, and it shall be satiate and made drunk with their blood: for the Lord GOD of hosts hath a sacrifice in the north country by the river Euphrates.

(Isa 13:5-7 KJV) They come from a far country, from the end of heaven, *even* the LORD, and the weapons of his indignation, to destroy the whole land. *{6}* Howl ye; for the day of the LORD *is* at hand; it shall come as a destruction from the Almighty. *{7}* Therefore shall all hands be faint, and every man's heart shall melt *(8)*, and they shall be afraid: pangs and sorrows shall take hold of them; they shall be in pain as a woman that travaileth: they shall be amazed one at another; their faces *shall be as* flames.

(Isa 2:11-12 KJV) The lofty looks of man shall be humbled, and the haughtiness of men shall be bowed down, and the LORD alone shall be exalted in that day. *{12}* For the day of the LORD of hosts *shall be* upon every *one that is* proud and lofty, and upon every *one that is* lifted up; and he shall be brought low:

(Rev 6:15-16 KJV) And the kings of the earth, and the great men, and the rich men, and the chief captains, and the mighty men, and every bondman, and every free man, hid themselves in the dens and in the rocks of the mountains; *{16}* And said to the mountains and rocks, Fall on us, and hide us from the face of him that sitteth on the throne, and from the wrath of the Lamb:

(Mat 24:30-31 KJV) And then shall appear the sign of the Son of man in heaven: and then shall all the tribes of the earth mourn, and they shall see the Son of man coming in the clouds of heaven with power and great glory. *{31}* And he shall send his angels with a great sound of a trumpet, and they shall gather together his elect from the four winds, from one end of heaven to the other.

This is the Day of the Lord.
Jesus told the high priest before the crucifixion he would see this day. All the dead shall see it. Math26v64
The bible says by the mouth of two or three witnesses let every matter be established.

David saw this day in its entirety.

(Psa 18:7-20 KJV) Then the earth shook and trembled; the foundations also of the hills moved and were shaken, because he was wroth. *{8}* There went up a smoke out of his nostrils, and fire out of his mouth devoured: coals were kindled by it. *{9}* He bowed the heavens also, and came down: and darkness *was* under his feet. *{10}* And he rode upon a cherub, and did fly: yea, he did fly upon the wings of the wind. *{11}* He made darkness his secret place; his pavilion round about him *were* dark waters *and* thick clouds of the skies. *{12}* At the brightness *that was* before him his thick clouds passed, hail *stones* and coals of fire. *{13}* The LORD also thundered in the heavens, and the Highest gave his voice; hail *stones* and coals of fire. *{14}* Yea, he sent out his arrows, and scattered them; and he shot out lightnings, and discomfited them. *{15}* Then the channels of waters were seen, and the foundations of the world were discovered at thy rebuke, O LORD, at the blast of the breath of thy nostrils. *{16}* He sent from above, he took me, he drew me out of many waters. *{17}* He delivered me from my strong enemy, and from them which hated me: for they were too strong for me. *{18}* They prevented me in the day of my calamity: but the LORD was my stay. *{19}* He brought me forth also into a large place; he delivered me, because he delighted in me. *{20}* The LORD rewarded me according to my righteousness; according to the cleanness of my hands hath he recompensed me. *Also 2Sam22v8-20*

Last Judgment / The Day of the Lord's completion and the fulfillment of the Second Coming.

Note: In Matt chapter 24:31 Jesus leaves us with the scene of his gathered elect.Rev.ch7 shows the martyrs resurrected before the Seventh Seal is opened. Yet the unjust are not resurrected until after the great earthquake and hailstorm of the seventh judgment in which they are killed.
The sealing of the 144,000 in Rev.7 takes place also before the seventh Judgment. I believe their sealing in Rev.7v3 was a supernatural preservation for them and those under their care. Because only by the protective hand of God could any one survive these calamities. This also means those with the mark will find no way to escape deaths grasp.

(Rev 8:1 KJV) And when he had opened the seventh seal, there was silence in heaven about the space of half an hour.

(Rev 8:5 KJV) And the angel took the censer, and filled it with fire of the altar, and cast *it* into the earth: and there were voices, and thunderings, and lightnings, and an earthquake.

(Job 37:4 KJV) After it a voice roareth: he thundereth with the voice of his excellency; and he will not stay them when his voice is heard.

(Rev 16:19 KJV) And the great city was divided into three parts, and the cities of the nations fell: and great Babylon came in remembrance before God, to give unto her the cup of the wine of the fierceness of his wrath.

(Rev 16:21 KJV) And there fell upon men a great hail out of heaven, *every stone* about the weight of a talent: and men blasphemed God because of the plague of the hail; for the plague thereof was exceeding great.

(Rev 14:20 KJV) And the winepress was trodden without the city, and blood came out of the winepress, even unto the horse bridles, by the space of a thousand *and* six hundred furlongs.

(Isa 34:2-4 KJV) For the indignation of the LORD *is* upon all nations, and *his* fury upon all their armies: he hath utterly destroyed them, he hath delivered them to the slaughter. {3} Their slain also shall be cast out, and their stink shall come up out of their carcasses, and the mountains shall be melted with their blood. {4} And all the host of heaven shall be dissolved, and the heavens shall be rolled together as a scroll: and all their host shall fall down, as the leaf falleth off from the vine, and as a falling *fig* from the fig tree.

(2 Pet 3:10) But the day of the Lord will come as a thief in the night; in the which the heavens shall pass away with a great noise, and the elements shall melt with fervent heat, the earth also and the works that are therein shall be burned up.

(Isa 24:19-20 KJV) The earth is utterly broken down, the earth is clean dissolved, the earth is moved exceedingly. *{20}* The earth shall reel to and fro like a drunkard, and shall be removed like a cottage; and the transgression thereof shall be heavy upon it; and it shall fall, and not rise again.

(Rev 19:20 KJV) And the beast was taken, and with him the false prophet that wrought miracles before him, with which he deceived them that had received the mark of the beast, and them that worshipped his image. These both were cast alive into a lake of fire burning with brimstone.

(Rev 14:11 KJV) And the smoke of their torment ascendeth up for ever and ever: and they have no rest day nor night, who worship the beast and his image, and whosoever receiveth the mark of his name.

(Rev 11:15 KJV) And the seventh angel sounded; and there were great voices in heaven, saying, The kingdoms of this world are become *the kingdoms* of our Lord, and of his Christ; and he shall reign for ever and ever.

(Rev 10:3 KJV) And cried with a loud voice, as *when* a lion roareth: and when he had cried, seven thunders uttered their voices.

(Rev 16:17 KJV) And the seventh angel poured out his vial into the air; and there came a great voice out of the temple of heaven, from the throne, saying, It is done.

(Dan 7:13-14 KJV) I saw in the night visions, and, behold, *one* like the Son of man came with the clouds of heaven, and came to the Ancient of days, and they brought him near before him. *{14}* And there was given him dominion, and glory, and a kingdom, that all people, nations, and languages, should serve him: his dominion *is* an everlasting dominion, which shall not pass away, and his kingdom *that* which shall not be destroyed.

……………………….. IT IS FINISHED.

Explore the book: J Sidlow Baxter.
Academic Book
1415 Luke drive
S.E. Grad Rupidge Michigan
49506 L C C C N 60 – 50187

Foundations of Pentecostal Theology
L.I. F.E. Bible College at Los Angele
L C C C N Box 8762 Zip Code 5084

ABINGDON'S STRONG'S
EXHAUSTIME CONCORDANCE
L C C C N B S 425.58. copyright 198(

Things to come.
J Dewright Penecost
Copyright 1958
1SBN 0-310 30890-9
Zandervan

The Seduction of Christianity
ISBN 0-89081-441-4
Harvest House Publishers
Eugene Oregon

Manners and Customs of the Bible
James M. Freemen
ISBN 0-888270-022-7
Logos International
New York

Nelson Quick Reference
William Smith, L.L.D.
Thomas Nelson Publishers
ISBN 0-847-6906-7

Quick Verse Parsons Tech.
Copyright 1996

Encarta. Encyclopedia 1998
Copyright 1997

Escape From the coming
Tribulation
Guy Duty
Copyright 1975
Bethany Fellowship Inc. ISBN 0-87123-131-Y

Late Great Planet Earth
Copyright 1970
ISBN 0-553—13003-X
Zandervan

Selective Scripture Index.

154

155

Revelation..cont
..v4-5...pg.77
v6...pg.79...v10-11...pg.115
v13..pg.141
v14-20...pg30...v14-19..pg.99
15v2...pg122...v2-3...pg.100
v2-4...pg135
16v3...pg.136..v12-16...pg.144
.v10-11..pg..142
.....v12....pg.45
v15..pg.33..v14-16.pg.43
v19-21.............pg.25
17v1..pg.94...v5-9..pg.92/ 94
v8,.11-13...pg.68/ 70
v11..pg.128
v12-13 &16....pg.14, pg72
v15...pg.94
18v1..pg.120
..v4-5,..9-10..pg.94/ 95
v20-21...pg.72
19v6-7...pg.45
v7-9, 17-18...pg.49
v11-16..pg.54..v20..pg.85
v20-21.pg.115
20v2.v5-7..pg.50
v4.....pg...101,141
v12...pg.34
.v15...pg52
21v1-4...pg.52
22v16...pg.16v/ 49